COBBES MEADOW
A story of riding with the disabled

By the same author:
I'm smiling as hard as I can. Mowbray, 1981.
Coping with Christian childbirth. Mowbray, 1982.
Mornings of joy – a Christian approach to pregnancy and childbirth.
    Kingsway, 1987.

COBBES MEADOW

A story of riding with the disabled

by

PENNIE KIDD

Foreword by Captain Mark Phillips

Illustrations by Joy Claxton

Buckland Publications Ltd.
125 High Holborn, London WC1V 6QA

*This book is dedicated to all riders and helpers of the
Cobbes Meadow Group of Riding for the Disabled Association, Kent.*

ISBN 0 7212 0915 7

Printed and bound in Great Britain by
Buckland Press Ltd., Dover, Kent.

CONTENTS

Pennie Kidd is an ex-nursing sister, clergy wife, and mother of three sons. Pennie has written an autobiography and a book on childbirth. She lives with her family in Canterbury, Kent.

FOREWORD
by Mark Phillips

It has to be said that I have been, to date anyway, one of the lucky ones. I've enjoyed good health all my life, and with my faculties have developed a very special relationship with the horse that has taken me to the four corners of the world and to the pinnacle of equestrian competition. From competitive success I have remained fortunate and been able to move into the fields of course designing and training that still allow me to work with horses on a daily basis all around the world.

Others have not been so fortunate. Through no fault of their own they have not been able to enjoy the use of all their faculties in the same way as me. It has not stopped them though having an extraordinary and richly rewarding relationship with that same and most remarkable and versatile of creatures.

I have been lucky enough to see the Riding for the Disabled Association (RDA) in action all around the world. Everywhere is the same, it seems that the horse knows its responsibilities when working with handicapped people.

The mental and often physical fortitude which disabled people are able to get from the warmth and movement of riding and the very special love and respect for their steed is a phenomenon at which I still marvel.

Pennie Kidd, an ex-nursing sister, once enjoyed the freedom of riding as a healthy child. Later in life she developed multiple sclerosis and experienced riding once again with the help of the RDA. This book gives us an intriguing insight into the mountains climbed and the rewards gained by handicapped riders and their often equally remarkable helpers and horses.

As teachers we often say riding horses is for everyone. This book is testament to that statement.

When reading this moving story, those that have ridden will understand the feelings and sensations of sitting on a horse and the camaraderie that develops amongst fellow horse people. Those that haven't may well feel they have missed something in life.

Mark Phillips

ACKNOWLEDGEMENTS

I wish to thank Maurice, my husband, for his constant encouragement, and for reading and checking the script. Thanks also to our three sons: Chris, Tim and Jon for their humour and patience. To Margaret Warland and Jill Relton my thanks for typing so willingly, and to Catherine McCully for help with research. Finally my appreciation to Joy Claxton for her enchanting illustrations.

INTRODUCTION

Writing this book seems a good way to express my deep appreciation to the Riding for the Disabled Association. It is a personal story which I hope will make the work of the RDA better known, and be an encouragement to riders and helpers alike. The RDA has given so much to so many over the years. Disabled riders have been enabled to develop trust and confidence, which have gone hand in hand with independence and enjoyment. To have four sturdy legs, a safe body and a sensitive mind through your horse is a valued experience for anyone who, through illness or injury, has lost confidence in their own bodies or minds. My hope is that helpers will pass on our thanks to the equine community, and that companionship will continue to flourish on all levels.

Pennie Kidd,
Canterbury, Kent.

Chapter One

FIRST RIDES

"Grip with your knees – you'll never ride if you don't grip with your knees." The lady's shrill voice clipped the breezy air in the stable yard. Her green wellington boots squelched on the oozing wet straw as she strode resolutely ahead of me, leading my weary little Shetland pony with its hollowed back and sagging belly. My young lean body lurched forward with each reluctant pace, my shoulders high and tense, my arms stiff and straight and my thin fingers clutching the rough shaggy mane falling divided over the pony's neck. Warm sunlight teased and played through branches of nearby lofty trees and leaves whispered and nodded in conferred agreement with the lady's instructions. A comforting moist breeze caressed my pale face, bringing the heavy scent of sweat and saddle. I was eight years old, and glowed with pride as I determined to become the greatest horsewoman of the day.

My first memory of a horse was that of the faithful old carthorse trundling down the bumpy lane in our quiet affluent Surrey village, pulling the milk cart. I would run out to look with awe at this immense animal, with its great clomping hooves, rough coat, and blinkered eyes. I loved animals, believing fiercely that they understood me. I kept rabbits with quivering enquiring pink noses, and two small soft trembling mice. Yet it was our young dog, Pip, a black and white cocker spaniel who was my closest and most trusted friend. Pip would sit and wait for me at the top of our gravel drive in a state of restless expectation as I dawdled slowly home from school. Then, almost home, I would run to hug him. With his tail wagging, his eyes aglow with happiness, he was hardly able to contain his excitement. With my arms around him I would push my face into his doggy coat, relishing the soft warm feel, the smell, the love; my satchel and my young cares momentarily cast aside. So it was that on my eighth birthday my mother keenly suggested that my sister and I should go riding. There was a small riding school in the village, and we could cycle there together on a Saturday morning. I was thrilled with the idea, imagining all the horses would resemble the milkman's horse. On the appointed Saturday we set off through the village to the riding school. My sister was far taller than me, being four years my senior, and I had great difficulty in keeping up with her as she sped down the stony lane, round the road past the ancient country church, along by the post office, and then extra fast down the long hill under tall spreading beech trees. At last, panting from our rush, we prised open the stiff heavy bolt on the dangling gate, and pushed our bikes down the hooved earthy track, and into the stable yard.

A large sleek, chestnut-coloured horse mildly objected to being tacked up, responding quickly to a firm command from the stable girl. A small fat brown pony stamped its hoof on the stone yard as it was given a final rub down, impatient now to be away. Horses' heads looked out curiously from stable doors, and all around people were busy. We left our bikes against an old shed and made ourselves known to the lady who seemed to be in charge. She gave us a quick friendly, efficient type of welcome, and immediately called to a fresh faced young girl to bring out Farthing for "the little one". Being called "the little one" wasn't new to me, but didn't exactly boost my confidence or my morale – after all, I was surely to become a rider of world renown. Farthing plodded across the yard, his gentle eyes barely visible beneath his mane. The little grey Shetland pony looked sympathetically at me, and I knew we were friends. A busy fly buzzed around Farthing's eyes, and I reached out carefully to brush it away. My small hand felt the rough coat, its slight greasiness, and I stroked it, sensing Farthing's pleasure at my simple action. The stable girl asked if I had ridden before – and, a little embarrassed, I answered shyly that I hadn't. She showed me the worn stirrup irons, and held the leather for me as I placed my foot on the shiny metal. "Now jump up and swing your leg over the saddle," said the girl smartly. I held tightly on to the saddle and pulled myself up awkwardly, leaning hard against the saddle. My leg swung over the pony's back, and with a less than graceful bump, I found myself sitting astride Farthing. I glanced around proudly, hoping my sister had seen my stylish mount – and felt a little humbled when I saw her already mounted on what seemed to be a very large and alert horse. The stable girl gave me the reins, winding them through my delicate fingers. It was at this point that the lady-in-charge exhorted me to grip with my knees as she took over from the stable girl and led my little pony over to her own horse. She mounted this magnificent looking animal, and with a light tug on the leading rein we set off, up the track, the other horses and riders following. I had been given a black riding hat to wear, which I found heavy and uncomfortable, but I felt excited and very nervous, my heart pounding, sure that one wrong move by me would send my pony galloping away over the fields, never to be seen again!

Farthing, I soon gathered, had been along this track many, many times. He stopped automatically at the large clanging gate, and started his slow laborious walk again without any instructions from me at all. He looked down at the furrowed mud all the time, and didn't seem to share my jittery delight at my first ride. I sat naturally straight, and tried to discover some kind of rhythm as my body wobbled back and forth. Once out of the gate the crisp sound of horses' hooves on the road thrilled me. We walked on, only turning at a point where a woodland path wound its way between silver birch trees away from the road, quietening the sound of the hooves. The ground here was soft grey sand, and the hooves sank deeply under us. The air was moist after a recent shower, and the latticed branches glistened with water drops. For a while I forgot my tension over trying to grip with my knees and hold the reins correctly. Just for a sublime moment I felt utterly at one with the damp sweetness all around me. The soft thud of the horses' hooves soothed me, the movement of the pony rocked me, and the sheer joy of riding, with the beauty of the woodland embraced my young spirit. I was happier than I'd been for years. The lady leading my pony frequently turned to ask if I was all right and would add some simple instruction. I began to like her. We carefully wound our way along the paths, until we came out on to a wide track, high up on a ridge, tufted with heathers. A sudden swirl of chill wind blew through my jacket. Farthing twitched his ear, lifted his head, and quickened his pace. "We'll try a little trot here," said the lady with the wellington boots. I clung on to Farthing's mane and the saddle, felt my toes sink down as my feet pressed ever more firmly into the stirrups, my back rounded, then suddenly I was shaking up and down, bumping unevenly in the saddle, sometimes landing on one side, then the other. My black hat bumped up and down too, occasionally obscuring my view completely. All I could think was to grip as hard as I could with my knees, which now felt sore, hot and painful. All too soon the trotting was over, and with flushed cheeks and puffing breath, I felt wonderful!

13

I patted Farthing and thanked him too.

Some of the other riders overtook us trotting and cantering along this high ridge overlooking distant steamy woodland hills. I envied the riders' ability, and wondered how on earth they rode with such ease. Soon the crackle of twigs accompanied our slow twisting walk back through the woodland path, the creamy wood anemones clustering together to share the woodland gossip. Suddenly the brightness of the sun on the wet road almost dazzled me after the shade from heavy overhanging branches. We were approaching the riding school. Through the gate, down the crumbly hoof-worn track, and we halted in the yard, my pony being handed to the stable girl, who took us over to a water trough. How I was to dismount was a total mystery to me – but in no time I was helped to release my foot from the stirrup iron, swing my leg over the saddle, and after what seemed like an enormous drop I was unsteadily feeling the hard ground beneath my feet again. I could have hugged Farthing and taken him straight home – however my childish dreams were interrupted as the lady-in-charge came and asked how I had enjoyed my first ride. "Wonderful," I answered and thanked her for her kindness. I patted Farthing and thanked him too, and told him in my heart that I would soon see him again; feeling he was going to miss me as much as I would miss him. My sister and I walked back to our bikes and cycled home. My bottom was sore, my legs ached, my hands were blistered, and my eyes shone with joy! I felt tired, refreshed and exhilarated.

It was many weeks before I rode again as, sadly, for some reason, riding lessons were never established as a regular feature. We were not a 'horsy' family, and I can only assume riding came low on my mother's list of priorities, with piano, violin and Scottish dancing lessons winning the day! In spite of this lack of continuity, each time I went to the riding school I met with that same thrill. Each time I rode Farthing, I was happier than ever, but alas, never gained significantly in riding skills, not even mastering the rising trot. Although I loved my attempts at riding, I never went through that phase of being horse 'crazy' like many young girls. Summer holidays were enjoyable. I have good memories of travelling by train to North Wales and spending idle days playing on the beach, walking for miles through the countryside and, of course, riding. We would go to a riding school in the next town along the coast. This was a very 'superior' riding school, with everyone turned out immaculately in boots, jodhpurs, shirt, tie and jacket. The horses were beautifully groomed, and the stable yard and tack room almost perfect. I remember watching the horses being tacked up, wondering which of these trim agile horses I would ride. There was a stone mounting block in the yard, and I would be helped to mount a suitable pony, then we would ride up a steep lane in single file. Although I enjoyed these rides, there was none of the thrill and love of riding that I had experienced in my own village This splendid pony had none of the affection of dear little Farthing, and although we may have looked very smart, I was, if truth be told, rather frightened. The land was very hilly and I had not the necessary balance or technique to cope with hills, and my natural apprehension made me tense and anxious. In spite of this, I wouldn't have missed this opportunity to ride.

School years followed, and I put all my youthful energy into studies and sport. There are many happy memories of playing in school lacrosse matches on bright frosty mornings at Guildford High. We were also encouraged to develop musical interests and I spent many hours singing in school choirs and the madrigal group. When I left school, I entered the nursing profession. I was grateful beyond measure for all such an excellent school had given me, and I felt well equipped to cope with the new challenges life would bring me. Little did I know then how hard those challenges were to be.

Chapter Two

A RISKY RIDER

Life as a student nurse was full of hard work, excitement and fun. I made many new friends, and most evenings the nurses' home was full of laughter and noisy music as we tried to shake off the responsibilities of the day on the wards.

The medical superintendent lived in a large house within the hospital grounds. His daughter, who was away at boarding school, owned her own pony called Lucky. A friend and I, with typical youthful abandon, and quite a lot of cheek, went to ask permission from the superintendent to groom and ride his daughter's horse! He seemed impressed by our nerve, and was only too pleased for someone to take an interest in the pony which, he confessed, was rather neglected. My friend had some knowledge of stable management and some riding experience but I, of course, had virtually none. One free sunny day I decided to ride Lucky. I donned jodhpurs and boots, yellow polo neck sweater and my black riding hat, and felt almost professional. Striding out across the field, I did rather wonder how I would manage Lucky but, with fond memories of Farthing in my mind, I had every confidence I would cope. Lucky was quietly grazing in a corner of the field and the stable door was shut tight. I unbolted it, and the sunlight lit up the stale dusty corners. Obviously the stable had not been in use for some time. Next to the stable was a dark tack room. A bridle hung lifelessly on a rusty hook. A saddle rested heavily on an old table, its shine dulled with dust and damp; a small square box lay in front of the saddle, with old rags, brushes and metal polish. So it was that, in total ignorance, I set about cleaning the tack. I rubbed and polished and shone all the leather and metal I could find – not knowing anything about its functions. Eventually most of the tack was clean, although I fear I had used too much saddle soap and not enough rub! My problem now was how to catch Lucky, and with what? A coarse simple head collar was hanging up beside the bridle. I took this and tried to work out just how it could fit on to a pony's head. Having satisfied myself that I knew how to apply it, I nervously left the tack room, head collar over my arm, and quietly approached Lucky. To my astonishment she ceased her munching of the delicious fresh grass, and wandered over to me. She was not too large and seemed glad to have some company.

Her coat was rough, and dried cracked mud clung to her side. I talked to her quietly; somehow instinct told me to be gentle and soothing. I stroked her neck and head, slipped the head collar over her ears and fastened the strap. Lucky stood quite still, perhaps knowing I hadn't a clue what I was doing. I praised her, and led her across the field to the stable. Not being able to find anywhere to tie her up I took her into the stable and closed the lower half of the door. I must admit I felt very thrilled with our achievement so far, for I knew it was a joint effort, or rather that Lucky should take more credit than I. Looking at the brushes, I had no idea which to use where, so I picked up the heavier brush and, talking quietly to Lucky, I began to brush away the dried mud on her coat, which shivered as I brushed. She seemed to appreciate my efforts. Sadly, I had no hay or sugar lumps with which to reward her or keep her occupied. The more I brushed, the more the air became dense with dust. A shaft of sunlight lit the frenzied dust particles, and I coughed and sneezed and Lucky blew hard from her nostrils. After a long time, I felt her coat looked good, and a final rub with a rag made a healthy shine appear.

I knew nothing of horses' shoes, so Lucky's hooves were not inspected or picked out. I went now to fetch the clean bridle, fortunately all correctly pieced together already, for I wouldn't have known how to assemble it. I raised one part up over Lucky's ears, carefully offered her the bit, and there it was – all looking good. I fastened a loose strap under her throat and left the reins loose over her mane. The saddle proved more difficult. I lifted the heavy leather into place on her back, but forgot the stirrup leathers, which caught under one side of the saddle. So, learning by my mistake, I repeated the action, this time with success. A flat broad strap fell down on the far side and I hoped this pulled under the pony's belly to keep the saddle on. Sure enough, there were small buckles which fastened this strap. Lucky looked at me kindly as if she could have taught me a thing or two – but I felt very pleased the exercise of tacking up had been relatively stress-free for both of us! As I knew nothing of neck straps or martingales, we did without.

Feeling a little more confident I led Lucky out of the stable into the clean clear air of a summer's day. Asking Lucky politely to stand still, I placed my foot into the stirrup iron, and swung up into the saddle. Not understanding how to check the girth, or adjust stirrup leathers, we set forth just as we were to walk round the field. Lucky nodded contentment, stopped here and there to munch a tasty morsel from the hedge, and behaved beautifully. Finding a little more courage, for I was certainly nervous, I gave a little kick with my heels and asked Lucky to trot. She seemed reluctant to do so, and I repeated the request, this time with success. Bumping up and down I clung on to the reins tightly. Lucky's head rose against my pull, and I felt myself slipping to one side. Trying to stop her, I pulled more, and slipped off the saddle, swinging quickly to the ground. Landing on my bottom, I instantly realised I was not hurt and simply suffered with hurt pride. The reins were stiff in my hand and Lucky, looking as surprised as myself, patiently stood still as I picked myself up and brushed myself down. Sensing my luck might run out, I led Lucky back to the stable, unfastened the girth, removed the saddle and bridle and with a reassuring pat turned my disbelieving pony out into the field again. It was an experience I shall never forget, and I can only feel that the heavens were smiling on me that day, for it could have led to a disaster for myself or Lucky, and I shudder at my foolishness.

I rode Lucky on a few occasions. She was such a placid pony that I felt safe on her. I even rode her through the hospital grounds and out on to the surrounding roads, returning quickly when I realised she was nervous on the road.

When I think of the risks I took in riding this little pony, I'm amazed. I was determined to manage a rising trot and, with no instruction, it was simply a matter of kicking lightly, asking for a trot and then trying to sort out the bumps which inevitably followed! Just occasionally I would rise and sit on the right time and I began to understand how much easier the trot felt when done a little more correctly. One day I went with my friend Pat and we tacked up together. Pat rode Lucky fast round the field adjacent to the stable. Lucky seemed to be in a naughty mood. She had been restless while being groomed and anxious being tacked up. Now Pat trotted her out into the field and, turning on the long side of the field, broke into a canter. Lucky had other thoughts and rushed close up to the fence where there were heavy low branches of overhanging trees. Suddenly there was a loud crack, Pat's riding hat spun off into the air and she fell heavily on to the bare earth under the trees. Lucky came to a halt some way off and I rushed over to help. Fortunately, Pat was all right but shaken. It had all happened so quickly, and again I felt we had been extremely lucky that neither horse nor rider was hurt.

On two occasions Pat and I drove to a nearby riding school and took horses out from there for two hours. It was a strange set-up, and I felt quite distinctly all was not well at this riding school. There seemed to be no proper organisation. We were allowed to ride out without anyone asking us if we were responsible and accomplished riders – which we certainly were not. We would take the horses, each about 15 hands, out on to the road and walk a long way alongside fast moving traffic before we came to a large and beautiful park where riding was permitted in certain areas. It was here I would practise my rising trot, but with no instruction I knew I was acquiring bad habits and I felt awkward and self-conscious. I knew I was not ready for such riding and one short attempt at a canter nearly put me off riding altogether. No, this riding was too risky. It was dangerous and irresponsible and I determined there and then not to ride again, not even on Lucky, until I had lessons and instruction.

It was seven years later that I was to ride again in very different circumstances. Much had happened in those years. I had gone to Nottingham to take further nursing training in a hectically busy general hospital. Following this I worked in a Surrey hospital as a Junior Ward Sister, pleased to be living in the south of England again. Next came training at Queen Charlotte's Maternity Hospital where I fell hopelessly in love with the babies!

While I had been in Nottingham I had met a priest called Maurice and had kept in touch with him. We were both living in London now and our relationship developed as we spent more time together. I began to realise I was very fond of him. At this time I went to spend a few days with my uncle and aunt in Sussex. During my stay, I booked up at a local riding school to have an hour's ride with instruction. I hadn't ridden for seven years and wondered how I would fare. Once at the school, a slender bay was brought to me. She looked very pretty and graceful and I felt privileged to ride her, particularly as I was aware of my riding being so poor. The instructor asked what riding experience I had and I told her I had ridden very little, feeling somewhat ashamed of my rides with Lucky.

On this ride I was placed midway in a line of about six horses and riders. We commenced our ride with a walk across fields, trekking carefully along a narrow path. I felt relaxed. The scent of the horses brought back fond memories of Farthing all those years ago and it made me realise the importance of first rides for a child. I felt more at ease now, riding amongst others, and with a good instructor. The views from high up on the Sussex Downs were magnificent, the cool air bringing a tingling refreshment. Somehow the horse's movement felt easier, and much to my delight, I managed a satisfactory rising trot. All too soon the ride was over but it had been a really good ride for me. I had felt at one with my horse, as if sharing my thoughts and feelings as I had as a little child on the rides in Claygate.

In February the following year I enjoyed a holiday with a friend, Anne. We drove north, shedding our cares and responsibilities with each mile, eventually arriving in the superb Yorkshire Dales. The air was keen and a thin winter sun bathed the landscape with muted winter colours. My heart leapt at the beauty of it all as I marvelled at the magnificent hills, streams, waterfalls and jagged crags soaring up into the sky. We were welcomed warmly at Scargill House, a Christian holiday centre and conference house near Kettlewell.

Along the dale there was a farm and riding school. I made enquiries and it was a few days later that I drove up the dale to this remote farm. A cheery welcome awaited me and I began to feel this ride was going to be good. The ponies were tough, rugged fell ponies with broad chests and short stocky legs, their black colouring contrasting with the faint winter colours of the landscape. My pony was called Banter. We eyed each other up and down. He was tough and strong and had a confident look in his eye. I took to him immediately, stroked his neck and patted him. The gentleman in charge of the ride helped all the riders to tack up and spoke enthusiastically about the abilities of the little ponies. Once mounted I felt strangely wrongly proportioned, my legs seeming to be too long for the pony, and the broad back gave a squat feeling I had not experienced before.

Nervous excitement flushed through me once more as we set out noisily through the stable yard, then softly over the springy, wet green turf of the lower foothills. The air was crisp and white breath blew back on my cold face. Banter strode out with certainty, obviously enjoying this morning ride. The sense of power from these ponies was felt with every stride. Soon our short line of ponies could be seen trekking high up the hillside. The path wound its way alongside a shallow stony stream, sparkling, dancing and splashing its way along the turbulent fast flowing route; rough grey crags faced out from the hillside. Banter quickened his pace; he leapt from crag to crag, hesitating a moment, then springing up to a higher level. It was thrilling as my legs gripped, and my body was pulled and pushed through the air, the broad back of the pony helping my balance and securing my seat. I had never ridden like this before and I trembled with effort and excitement. A low cloud now shrouded the sloping shoulders of the hills, the misty air clinging damply around us. It was cold but I felt warm inside my thick pullover and jacket.

In so many ways this holiday and especially this ride were a turning point in my life. As we left behind the chill mist of the hills, the sun shone persuasively through the white mist. I thought of Maurice, and knew that I loved him, and wanted to share my life with him. We trekked down the hillside, our bodies leaning back heavily to counter the drop of the ponies' heads as they carefully climbed down from crag to grass. Sure-footed and proud these delightful ponies carried us back towards the farm, the sky clearing as we quickly descended. Soon the wide farm gates embraced us and we walked into the stable yard. I think that ride had been special for all of us and I took my time to say thank you to Banter as he keenly pulled hay from a net. I said farewell to the others as we all left to go our separate ways.

After a romantic few months, Maurice and I were married in a tiny chapel in London. Blissfully happy and full of that special sense of adventure, we flew to Crete for our honeymoon to the welcoming warmth of the sun.

The following few years were spent very happily and busily in the small parish of Hanworth in Middlesex. We began our home in a huge old rectory in acres of grounds! To our absolute delight our first son Christopher was born after a healthy pregnancy. We added to our family without delay, and next year Timothy was born, followed closely by Jonathan. We were wonderfully happy with our three boys. Altogether life was very good.

It was a few years later that difficulties arose. One day I noticed a tight feeling around my arm which wouldn't go away. Within hours my feet felt tingly, this strange feeling spreading to my legs. After a while my sense of balance seemed all wrong and I found it difficult to walk

I thought of Maurice and knew that I loved him.

properly. I felt extremely tired and very anxious. These symptoms persisted and, with my nursing knowledge, I put two and two together and feared I could have multiple sclerosis. My doctor made an appointment for me to see a professor of neurology in London. I was admitted to the National Hospital for Nervous Diseases, Queens Square, where I had a week of tests and examinations. Eventually the professor came to my bedside and told me that in his opinion I did have multiple sclerosis.

Maurice and I were shocked and stunned, and yet relieved that a diagnosis had been made. Now I could begin the long readjustment in my life. The boys were still very young, and it was important that life for all the family should continue as normally and happily as it had always been. Maurice was wonderful in his total support and care, and we gradually began to face the fears and hopes of the future. We cried a lot, laughed a lot, and prayed a lot and gradually the anxiety lessened, and we came to terms with my weak legs and tiredness.

We had now been in this parish nearly ten years, and we began to feel a move might be right for the family. After a short time we were offered a new living in Kent. Sad to leave our friends, but excited by the thought of new pastures, we prepared to leave, finally moving just after Christmas. As we drove down the motorway towards Kent, I thought back over the years which had been creative and fulfilling. I was now registered as disabled and I wondered what the future held for us. The boys were still so young and I worried lest we couldn't cope with my illness. Leaving friends before you've had time to make new ones is always hard, but with difficulties to face, somehow it seemed harder than ever. I also wondered if I would be able to ride again. I had seen the address of Riding for the Disabled in Middlesex, and not knowing quite what it was I made some enquiries, only to be told it was for the Star and Garter soldiers. Riding was something I had missed over the past years, but then how could I ride now I could hardly walk? Soon we drove near to Canterbury, the countryside becoming more beautiful with each mile as we approached the village of Chartham, though the earth was held rigid in frosty cold. We travelled on through fields and woodland, often passing horses in fields, looking cold in their winter rugs and missing the lush pastures of spring and summer. No, I had come to terms with the fact that I would not be able to ride again, that must be something of the past now. In no time we arrived at our large rectory and were immediately made to feel very welcome. New friends came to meet us, some even brought pies and hot meals to help us out over the next few days. Our new home was set in two acres of wild garden, up on the side of a valley, with superb views across the village and towards hills. I revelled in this country, drinking in each detail. The parish of Chartham was small and the church was the dominant feature of this country village, set in outstanding country, near to Canterbury. The move was made easy by the friendship shown to us, and soon we felt at home as we sat in front of a crackling open log fire in the lounge. We felt very fortunate to have this beautiful place in which to live and work.

Within a month of our move, a very kind lady in the parish was telling me various things about the village and the countryside around. She asked me if I ever rode horses. Feeling rather sore, I explained it was something I had enjoyed in the past but now I didn't feel able to ride any more. She explained to me that just four miles away in a neighbouring village, there was a group of the Riding for the Disabled Association. She told me then how special helpers and instructors who know and understand what it means to be disabled, helped disabled people of all ages to enjoy riding, with whatever assistance they may need. The lady gave me the name of the person in charge, so that I could make my own enquiries. I thanked her and returned home full of excitement and not a little disbelief about all I had heard. If there really was riding for the disabled, then I wanted to become part of it and I set about my enquiries right away.

Chapter Three

COBBES MEADOW

"Yes," said the pleasant voice on the telephone, "you'll need a doctor's certificate before you can ride, but do come and see what we do." So it was that one very wet February day Maurice drove me to Waltham, a tiny village some four miles across the beautiful downs, now bare and chill in brown and grey. We found the riding school easily and parked the car in a large open area. I pulled myself from the car seat and steadied myself with my stick. I couldn't see any horses, and wondered just where I should go.

As I turned, a friendly clear voice called out, "Hello, are you Mrs. Vicar?" I smiled broadly, and saw a slim attractive lady approaching across the grooved muddy ground. This was Jenny, the chairman of the Cobbes Meadow branch of the RDA. It was good to meet her and to be made so welcome. She took my arm and guided me carefully across the mud, and around the large rippling puddles which reflected the cold grey sky. We walked towards a large indoor riding school with huge heavy wooden doors. Yellow straw was beaten into the ground, and the smell of horses and hay warmed my spirit and brought back many happy memories.

The Cobbes Meadow Branch of the RDA was started in April 1972 by two dedicated people who raised funds for the group by running keep-fit classes! The Chaucer Riding School at Waltham kindly allowed the group to use its premises on one day a week. At that time there were just five riders in the class. As interest grew, more helpers joined and more riders contacted the group, wanting to ride and to have instruction. It became increasingly obvious that facilities needed to be expanded, and a pipe-dream developed of the group one day having their own indoor riding school. For the time being however, much appreciation was felt towards the Chaucer Riding School for their kindness.

Jenny took me to sit on a bench just inside the riding school. She introduced me to Lynne, the trim neat chief instructor who also welcomed me. I felt instantly I could trust and have confidence in her. Other people glanced at me as they helped tether a horse or talk to a rider, and gave me warm smiles. I began to relax, but felt rather bewildered as I tried to understand what people were doing. Everyone looked so busy. I noticed some people walking with sticks or crutches, all wearing jodhpurs and boots and various types of jackets. Some had navy blue sweat shirts on with a picture of a pony and rider being led by a helper. The words 'Riding for the Disabled' surrounded the picture. The school was very large, with a track beaten in the dark peat passing boards with various letters on. Horses were being tacked up, and riders were being helped to mount. I noticed that even riders who couldn't walk too well, seemed to ride with some style and balance. I felt encouraged, but wondered how I would cope now my legs were weak and lacked co-ordination.

This was the first time since my diagnosis was made that I was mixing with other disabled people. I was suddenly aware of the 'us' and 'them' situation. I was now classed as disabled, the helpers were all fit and well. I felt strangely alone although the people around me were so friendly. Someone came and sat down beside me. She said her name was Sheila, and she was a helper here, her son Peter being a rider. I wondered which rider Peter was, but appreciated Sheila's welcome and interest. I explained I couldn't ride yet, but had come to see what went on at Cobbes Meadow. Sheila left to help a rider to mount from a mounting block. A large bay stood patiently waiting for the rider to settle comfortably on his back. The riders began their ride at a walking pace around the school in single file, with Lynne watching carefully and giving encouragement to both horses and riders. I was impressed and thought back to my early rides as a child. It was cold now, and I rubbed my legs with my hands hoping to create some warmth.

Suddenly the quiet of the school was broken as a group of men arrived. They were dressed for riding, but it was fairly obvious to a trained eye such as mine, that they were mentally handicapped. Friendly hands enthusiastically offered to shake mine, and faces alive with enthusiasm and enjoyment came and told me their names and asked for mine. I tried to be relaxed and friendly in return, but felt a deep tension within me. Here I was, disabled, now sitting alongside both physically and mentally disabled people. Up to now I had still thought of myself as a ward sister, mother, clergy-wife – but disabled, no. This was a new challenge which hurt. It hurt to realise I needed help just like the other riders. It hurt that I wasn't one of the helpers, bright and healthy. It hurt that I needed reassurance and encouragement. For a moment I wanted to run away, to leap up and break out of this school running as fast as my legs would carry me back to Maurice and the safety of the car and home.

The moment of panic brought a lump to my throat, but I quickly relaxed again as Jenny came back to me and asked if I was enjoying it. "Yes," I answered, unsure of the truth of it, and I smiled nervously. Jenny told me I would ride Susie if I came next week, and pointed out a slim skewbald horse, gently and patiently carrying her rider, a man with glasses, who I gathered was called Charles and who also had multiple sclerosis. Maurice came to find me now, and suggested we should go home as I was feeling cold. I thanked Jenny, and promised I would get the doctor's form signed, and that I would return next week for my first ride. Maurice helped me back over the mud and stones of the yard. There was so much to think about, so much I had seen and felt. I shared many of my feelings with Maurice as we drove along the winding woodland lanes. I was full of doubts and questions, but I was also excited at the prospect of riding again, and greatly encouraged by the friendliness and warmth I had felt amongst riders and helpers at Cobbes Meadow.

"Mrs. Kidd?" asked a neatly dressed gentleman at the surgery. This I realised must be my new doctor. I had come to the surgery for the first time to ask my doctor to sign the RDA form. I clumsily stood up, and followed slowly to the consulting room. Soon I was trying to explain to a very pleasant doctor that I wanted to go riding. Yes, I did have multiple sclerosis and yes, I did want to go riding! Did I detect a look of disbelief, or was it faint amusement? How did I think riding would help me, asked my new doctor, by now probably wondering what sort of new patient he had taken on. I explained that I felt I would enjoy it, and hoped it would help my sense of balance, and possibly help to strengthen the weak muscles of my legs. All this was duly written down on the RDA form to which he added his signature with a flourish. Relieved, and seeing the funny side of this interview, I gave my new doctor a broad grin and wobbled out of his consulting room!

The following Monday, dressed somewhat inappropriately in jeans and sweater and walking shoes, I drove with Maurice to Waltham, clutching my doctor's form. The trees were rigid with cold, and a faint wintry sun flicked between the bare branches. A richly coloured pheasant ran awkwardly from a hedge and across the road, doubtless cursing the invention of the motor car. It flapped away into a roughly ploughed field, the soil glistening wet in long restful furrows. Arriving at Cobbes Meadow, we parked the car and, as I got up from the seat, I was welcomed by Charles. We soon chatted about riding and Charles reassured me how safe it all was and how Lynne would help me to ride again. As we entered the school I noticed Susie, tied up to the side of the school waiting patiently for her new and nervous rider.

Jenny was helping another lady to mount, and soon came over to me, glad I had returned. I gave her the doctor's note, and she led me towards the mounting block. Sheila untied Susie and brought her over to me, encouraging her to stand still alongside the steps. A dark haired happy-looking girl introduced herself at this point; her name was Catherine and I later discovered she was the vice-chairman of the group. I felt incredibly nervous and rather self-conscious about my jeans, when everybody else seemed to be dressed in jodhpurs. I placed my unsure foot on the first step and soon rose to the height of the horse's saddle. Sheila and Catherine held me firmly and helped me to put my foot into the stirrup iron. I tried to raise my leg over the horse's back and with some gentle help soon found myself sitting astride Susie.

We were led out into the yard and a fair-haired girl took over, leading Susie gently forward. She told me her name was Rosemary and that one of her horses was in the school. We would be going for a short walk through some fields to get me used to the feel of riding again with another rider and helper. I felt tense and clumsy and clutched on to the front of the saddle with both hands. My shoulders and neck strained with excited anxiety. Rosemary happily asked me if I was all right and I told her how strange it felt, but that I was enjoying it. Susie's hooves clipped loudly across the cold hard lane, then we passed along a country track and through a field. By now my legs were beginning to feel tight and heavy, my feet seeming to do as they liked rather than work to give aid to Susie. I felt a little dismayed thinking I would not get further than being led at a walk, but then I'd always been an impatient soul and wanted to run before I could walk! The views across the Kent countryside were softly inspiring, pale grey and blues and greens blending together in the thin hint of sun. The cold air made my skin tingle. My black hat didn't fit too well and moved slightly with my irregular movement. Susie seemed tired as she drooped her head and I thanked her for so carefully taking me on my first ride at Cobbes Meadow. Rosemary chatted happily and encouraged me to sit up straight, and try to rely on the reins rather than holding the saddle. We turned and started back. I had thoroughly enjoyed the ride, but doubted my ability to be able to ride to the standard I sought.

Maurice was pleased to see me safely back and watched as the helpers skilfully taught me how to dismount back on to the mounting block. Once my feet took my weight again my legs shook uncontrollably for a while and I felt rather stupid, only comforted by the helpers' reassuring and calm attitude. Lynne came over to me smiling broadly and asked Rosemary and me how we had fared. We had both enjoyed it and I told Lynne I looked forward to being able to ride a lot more. Before my next ride I visited the local saddlery and bought jodhpurs and boots. The assistants in the shop looked surprised as I asked for the requirements and, seeing their queries, I explained I rode with Riding for the Disabled. They were most encouraging and wished me well as I went on my way.

Over the following weeks I returned to Cobbes Meadow each Monday morning. The barren winter countryside gradually changing to a mantle of light green as leaves opened, coaxed by the gentle warmth of the spring sun. Bluebells vied for favour in the woodlands and clothed the ground with a rich misty blue. As I came to know Sheila and Rosemary, Lynne, Catherine and Jenny and others, I started to relax more and began to learn about riding correctly. We soon learned I was better mounting and dismounting without the mounting block, something I was particularly pleased about. A helper would lower the stirrup iron fully, help me place my foot in the iron, then with a mighty heave would push me up, another helper clearing my leg over the saddle. Lynne soon had me holding the reins correctly, I began to gain some sense of balance over the weeks and stopped holding the saddle, perhaps linking my thumbs under the neck strap instead. Lynne was always so careful, so thorough in checking for safety at every moment. I felt safe and could concentrate on trying to keep a good riding position. Keeping heels down was a problem as I couldn't feel properly where my heels were, but Lynne helped me to realise that if I sat correctly and pressed lightly down through my knees, then my heels would drop down and I could obtain a straight line through shoulders, hips and ankles. It was thrilling to be taught so well. Lynne would stop the ride (now always in the riding school) and ask us the correct aids for the walk, or halt. We would

It was thrilling to be taught so well.

practise each movement over and over again before going on to ride some sort of game which was fun and exciting.

One Monday morning while at Cobbes Meadow, Jenny asked me to ride out into the yard where I was to take my first test. I didn't know anything about tests, but happily agreed. Jenny asked me to walk slowly around the yard, and then asked me some very basic questions like the name of the saddle and bridle and stirrups. She asked me what the horse's nose was called and how we should describe what Susie wore on her feet. This was nice and basic and I knew the correct answers to all she asked me, with the exception of what we should call the deepest part of the saddle. I looked blankly at Jenny who kindly mouthed 'seat' – "Seat," I said brightly! We laughed, and Jenny assured me I had just passed my first test! I was given an RDA badge and a blue felt to pin behind it – and I felt great! Some months later, after learning a little more about horses, I was able to pass the second test for the red felt and followed this fairly quickly by gaining the third test, or green felt. By now I was becoming acquainted with the correct aids for the halt, walk and trot, and could name the main points of the horse, and knew some very elementary stable management and basic care. At this time Rosemary, one of the helpers, who looked after Grace, a grey horse I found rather broad, asked me to her home to ride Grace in the forest-land nearby. I drove out to the depths of the countryside and met Rosemary. She tacked Grace up and rode her out to the magnificent pine forest nearby and I followed in the car. The forest was massive and made the bridle paths dark between the rows of trees. The scent of the pine was superb. After a while Rosemary suggested I rode and she led Grace, just to be extra safe. I was glad, as I found Grace hard work, but today, out in the open, Grace moved beautifully, and a long trot gave me a real opportunity to work at a rising trot; it felt good. I was thrilled to be riding here amongst these grand trees; somehow a horse seemed the most appropriate way of travelling. It was a beautiful experience and one I shall long remember.

Some weeks we would sit in a little shed together and learn about horses, handling and trying to learn the names of parts of the tack. I had managed a rising trot after weeks of bumping up and down in the saddle, eventually learning by saying to myself "Clip-clop, clip-clop, up-down, up-down," over and over again, and the ride amongst the pine trees had helped so much. The problem was my legs were weak and my balance poor. However, by the time I took the green felt test I was able to maintain a rising or sitting trot, so I felt I was at last making progress. I was also getting to know the other riders, especially Charles and Pam, a lady who always seemed to ride particularly well. I would watch Charles and Pam carefully, trying to pick up some tips, then after the ride we would compare notes and, amidst much laughter, help each other to master some new technique or useful piece of knowledge.

Charles had always lived in Kent, having been born and brought up in Margate. He was evacuated at the age of eleven to Staffordshire and at fourteen left school to become a telegraph boy with the post office. He did national service in the Royal Air Force and quite enjoyed it. He returned to the post office as a sorting clerk and was soon promoted to postal officer. Charles married Maureen when he was twenty-six, and it was actually on his wedding day that he developed pins and needles in both legs. He was a very active young man, playing tennis, swimming, and walking for miles as well as playing with his two small children. The pins and needles became worse and when Charles was twenty-nine he went to his doctor. He was sent for tests at the hospital, and saw a neurologist who told Charles the problem was a trapped nerve, which would be better in ten days! Soon Charles developed numbness in his hands and his right arm and had a strange cold sensation. Charles was promoted and went to live in Canterbury. He was put on a job preparing for the publication of a post-code directory. This involved walking postman's deliveries all over East Kent. He enjoyed the work but couldn't understand why he kept feeling so extremely tired, after having been very fit. By 1973 Charles could only be described as feeling wretched.

He saw another consultant who examined him thoroughly at home, and concluded Charles had neuritis. Charles returned to his own doctor who told him it was multiple sclerosis. Charles felt shocked, he knew it was serious, but didn't know what it was or meant. He joined the Multiple Sclerosis Society, and he and Maureen learned all about the disease through their literature. Charles was now promoted again to a Postal Executive Officer but the anxiety over his health and the stress of the job made Charles ill again and he suffered a relapse, with difficulty in walking, loss of balance, double vision and dizziness. He was away from work for five months. Cortisone, the anti-inflammatory drug, did not help Charles, but eventually better health came and he returned to full-time work. Later, in 1979, Charles had another relapse with very similar symptoms and had to retire from work.

Charles is a man who enters into things fully and always seeks opportunities to help others. He joined the local MS Society and became its treasurer. The secretary of RDA, Tricia, had asked if there were any MS members who would like to ride – and so it was that Charles found himself going to Waltham for his first ride. He had never ridden a horse and knew nothing about them. However, there had been much talk of horses in Charles' childhood in the family, as his father was in the horse artillery and his grandfather would help to beach the lifeboat with the help of horses. He was a fly driver – a horse cab driver. When Charles first rode he was surprised how unsteady he felt and how poor his balance was. Under Lynne's excellent instruction Charles made good, if slow, progress. He really enjoyed it but never felt he was any good. Charles feels that riding with the RDA gives him a tremendous interest and sense of achievement. He says that for him to be able to sit on an animal that is bigger and stronger than he is, to be able to comfort it and get it to do what he wants, makes him feel very satisfied. The greater the challenge, the greater the satisfaction. Charles has made many friends through the RDA. He told me he felt that the people in RDA had done more to help him than anyone else in his life. He feels that RDA helpers go out of their way to help and ask nothing in return – come to think of it, that sounds a bit like Charles himself. Although Charles knows that his condition at the moment is slowly deteriorating, he is always cheerful and fun. He has enjoyed marvellous holidays with RDA in Wales and, as he cheerfully states, he's had some good falls!

One week at the school we had a real sadness to face as Susie, the skewbald I had ridden on my first rides at Cobbes Meadow, had to be put down after going lame. We had all become so fond of the horses, we sorely missed old Susie. I was now to ride Grace whom I had ridden with Rosemary in the pine forest. She was 15 hands and was rather broad. I must admit I found Grace difficult to ride. She had a lovely temperament and was so willing, but my legs ached and shook as I tried to kick her on and, when we had accomplished a trot together, it was hard to pull her back and stop her. "Feel on the reins" felt like the understatement of the year – as Grace trotted on until she decided to stop! My riding wasn't good enough to be able to know how to handle Grace who was just too strong for me to manage. I began to feel a little disheartened and wondered if my legs couldn't cope with any more riding. Sometimes I would ride Dreamer, a delightful 14 hands palomino. Dreamer was most attractive, holding his head well and being light to handle. He was, without doubt, my favourite though he was a little small for me. Soon

Lynne encouraged us to complete simple dressage tests. We all enjoyed these, watching each other carefully to see just how accurate we could become. Pam always seemed to do best, and Charles did well. Altogether riding was becoming great fun and I was certain it was helping my legs to grow stronger and improving my balance. I had, in one year, made many new friends, passed three felts and considerably improved my riding and knowledge about dressage and stable management.

It was at about this time that another helper joined us. A keen, cheerful, hardworking lady called Anthea arrived and brought with her a truly gorgeous horse named Sherry. Sherry (Scheherazade) was a part-bred Arabian mare; a 15 hands bright bay with two white socks. Sherry had competed in all pony club and riding club activities, invariably in the prize money, such as hunter trials, working hunter pony, eventing, show jumping and gymkhana. Sherry had hunted a great deal and still loved to go hunting. She had a kind and gentle nature and had taught countless numbers of children and adults to ride. Her performance record showed she was tremendously brave, indefatigable and always full of energy. She played a great part in RDA and on two occasions had entered for the Lloyds Bank RDA Championship, on each occasion being highly commended.

I felt immensely privileged when I was asked if I would like to ride Sherry. After Sheila helped me mount Sherry, I walked around slowly and carefully under the watchful eye of Lynne. In a moment I realised that Sherry needed only the slightest aid and she would obey. She was very comfortable. At the trot she had a good smooth pace and came back to walk as soon as she was asked. I could hardly believe how much easier it was to ride Sherry and felt very excited. Pam and Charles both rode Sherry over the next week or two and we all felt the same about her. Lynne encouraged me to try a few strides of canter, after making sure I understood exactly what aids to give. I was to ask on a bend, allow with the reins, press lightly with my inside leg on the girth and outside leg just behind the girth. Feeling very nervous and excited, trotting at an even pace, I asked for canter. Sherry obeyed instantly, the different rhythm taking me completely by surprise, I clung on, gripped with my legs and held the neck strap. Then I came back to trot and was pleased to hear Lynne praising both Sherry and me for a good effort.

It was planned in the summer of 1982 that we should all be taken to Hever Castle for a large area dressage competition for the Riding for the Disabled Association. The day dawned and the skies filled with ominous-looking clouds. Jenny picked Pam and me up in her car; Charles, Peter and his friend Stephen were being taken by Sheila. Anthea was to come with Sherry and Catherine would come with Dreamer. Other helpers came with food and drinks and as the sky darkened we set out for Hever. The drive took about an hour and a half and we nearly became lost amongst the dripping little lanes around Hever. Eventually we arrived, except for Anthea who had become even more lost but she arrived a little later. By now the rain was falling hard and we sat in the car, hearing the beating of the rain on the roof. The competition started and we watched various riders compete in the dressage at differing levels of competence. I felt worried that I wouldn't do too well, but then we all felt the same and nervously helped each other to overcome our fears.

Then it was my turn to mount Dreamer and walk around before hearing the horn blow on the judge's car which indicated they were ready for me. My heart was beating ten to the dozen and I felt tense, desperately trying to remember the dressage test. Suddenly the horn blew – that was it, no time for nerves now. I walked Dreamer down towards the dressage ring. I entered at 'A' and walked a straight line to 'X', halted, saluted (and I remembered to smile!). I walked on, trying not to 'fall in' at the corners, trotted on, wondering if my position was good enough. There was a moment of panic as I couldn't remember whether it was a ten or twenty metre circle – I trotted a 'twenty metre' and hoped it was right. I couldn't think what shape my circle ended up as, but then remembered just in time to walk across the ring, halt, and count slowly to six, completely still. Good old Dreamer must have known this was a special occasion and stood square and very still. On now, and a fast trot round to 'A' and up to 'X' then walk, then stop, trembling now with tension – salute and smile, and walk out on a long rein. What a thrill it had been – so nerve-racking and yet such fun. Soon, with the rain still blowing in waves across the field, we sat in the car and enjoyed a magnificent picnic, with wine, quiche and strawberries and cream, which the helpers had produced.

We joked and teased and laughed. Later in the wet afternoon, in torrential rain, I joined in a Handy Hunter competition. It was very exciting trying to race over a course, including some cavalletti which I'd never ridden over before. Dreamer was magnificent and obviously enjoyed it enormously. By now we were soaking wet, the rain dripping from the brim of my hat, my shirt and red tie all blotchy, and the smart black jacket Jenny had lent me, wet through. Somehow the rain didn't really matter, we were so caught up in the fun and excitement of the day. Back in the car we could hear the distant echoing sound of a loud speaker, apparently announcing the results of the dressage competition. Someone rushed up to the car and congratulated me – "What for?" I asked, and then heard to my astonishment that I had won first prize in the dressage and Pam had come second! We couldn't believe it. We could only think of our nervous rides and wondered what the judges had liked about them! "Well done, Dreamer," I thought; he had been so obedient and lovely to ride. There was much rejoicing as other riders had won various events and I had also come fifth in the Handy Hunter. People gathered now in one area of the field for the prize-giving. There was one marvellous incident we still laugh about. Peter had entered for the Handy Pony Event. He rode Dreamer and was led by Jenny. All went well, in spite of the pouring rain, until Peter and Dreamer jumped the cavalletti. Dreamer suddenly decided to take off with a huge jump and then run on, sensing he'd had enough. Jenny fell over and aquaplaned on her stomach over the squelching grass as she hung on to the leading rein with Dreamer making off! One of the VIP gentlemen spectators called out "Let go, you silly woman!" while Jenny shouted to Peter to "Pull, pull!" Peter was quite oblivious to all this kerfuffle and was happily enjoying his ride, while everyone around was collapsed in laughter!

Lady Astor was giving the prizes. Jenny pushed me in my wheelchair up to Lady Astor, who shook my hand and presented me with a lovely shield, then Pam received her rosette. We felt thrilled to bits, very wet and supremely happy for Cobbes Meadow as well as for ourselves. We knew it was the helpers' dedication, Lynne's superb instruction and the horses' impeccable manners which had won the shield and other awards, and we rejoiced all the way home.

Chapter Four

FUN AND FALLS

"Now then madam, how would you lead a pony?" The examiner stared down at me and I almost shook under his gaze. "I'd raise the stirrups, hold the leading rein in the right hand, close to the pony's head, and hold the other end of the rein in my left hand," I blurted out. Charles, Pat and I were not enjoying our fourth test for our Yellow felt, while Pam was taking her Bronze Award. Our examiner didn't appear to be enjoying it either. "All right, what's in these buckets?" I looked down at the samples of horses' bran, oats, nuts and barley. I'd little idea which was which, and hoped desperately Charles or Pat would know the answer. Things were not going well. "How do you hold a saddle?" This time Pat answered for us, correctly. "What are the aids for the trot?" The examiner took a long deep breath, I can't think what he thought of us. Next we had to ride round and demonstrate walk, and rising trot. "Go on, Madam," he shouted at me, "show me a canter." I knew that wasn't in the Yellow felt questions, and I was aware of feeling angry that I had been asked to demonstrate something I was not sure of. I asked Sherry to canter on the next bend, and fortunately she was as good as gold, so I cantered round the track, hoping my style was good enough for this abrupt examiner. Feeling we must have all failed, we were told, in turn, to dismount. The others having accomplished this, it was my turn. Like the others, I was used to having a helper who would help my leg over the saddle, and another to steady me once on the ground. "No, no, no – do it on your own!" My heart thumped, and I explained that I usually had help – but all to no avail. The helpers stood by and watched, unable to help. I leant forward, slowly and awkwardly releasing my feet from the stirrups, and then very, very slowly, eased my right leg over the saddle. It was almost impossible. I felt so angry and anxious. My face flushed, I fought back tears. My leg seemed stuck on the cantle. Eventually, with tremendous effort, I managed to free it, and I slid quickly to the ground. Clinging on to the saddle – my legs shook, more with rage than weakness. The examiner seemed satisfied I had done as he instructed, but I felt it had been an unnecessary exercise. The fact that we had all passed the Yellow felt and Pam had passed her Bronze, was some compensation, but the experience of this exam had upset me, but undeterred, I determined to work for future exams.

I had been impressed by Pam's riding, and her sense of determination to ride well. Pam needed to use crutches to get around, but once she was mounted on Sherry, or Polly whom she usually rode, then she looked the picture of health, and had a certain poise about her which was impressive.

Pam had been brought up in London, and experienced a normal and happy childhood, though she confessed she didn't enjoy school. Her real love was dancing. Pam married at nineteen, and there followed good years, including the birth of four children. Dancing dominated her life, she was a specialist in Highland Dancing, a more advanced form of Scottish dancing. Pam toured the British Isles teaching and instructing, she even taught the Scots how to dance! When Pam was forty-three, she tripped and fell on a piece of torn linoleum in an office. The consequences of this fall were horrific. Pam had broken the neck of the large thigh bone, the femur. The bone was pinned, and after three weeks Pam left hospital on crutches. She was never to walk again without the aid of those crutches.

Complications arose, and six months later further surgery actually made the hip worse. After three years of immobility and pain, an operation was performed to place a metal rod in the joint, but this operation failed and a partial hip replacement operation was carried out. As if all this wasn't enough, this last operation was also unsuccessful, and just eighteen months later a total hip replacement was performed. During the course of this operation a nerve was compressed, and caused paralysis of the right leg.

Pam told me she has never felt bitter about what happened but has simply tried to take things in her stride. Obviously she was profoundly disappointed, and she felt that a shutter had been pulled down in her life. She could no longer dance, no longer even walk without aid. Fortunately Pam had a fighting spirit and this prevented her from becoming depressed. She involved herself with housework, but there was an emptiness now, and part of her felt dead inside.

One day Pam happened to go to her nearest Citizens' Advice Bureau over some advice she needed, and quite by chance read a notice about Riding for the Disabled. She had always wanted to ride as a child but her mother never allowed it as her sister had once been kicked by a horse. Pam wrote down the telephone number and as soon as she arrived home she telephoned the secretary, who was then a charming lady called Tricia. Pam felt very conscious of her age, after all, she was fifty-three now, and quite expected to be told she was too old to ride! Only words of encouragement were expressed, and Tricia told her all about RDA and how it could help. Without delay Pam persuaded her doctor to fill in the medical form, and then went along to Waltham for her first ride. I asked Pam how she felt about that ride – "Wonderful, absolutely terrified!" she exclaimed. She said how the experience of even sitting on a horse was so totally different from how she had expected. She was so frightened, there was a helper to lead, a helper each side, and a helper behind her and her horse! With only partial feeling in her right foot, Pam found giving the correct aids very difficult, and soon learned to compensate with her hands on the reins and her voice to communicate to the horse.

Once Pam had found her confidence, she was a natural rider, and had little difficulty in mastering a rising trot and the canter. She went with the RDA on some wonderful holidays, and laughs at one unforgettable experience. She had collected a new pair or glasses the day before her holiday. The following day these glasses were brushed off her face by a twig – and lo and behold, the horse trod on them and they broke into masses of tiny pieces! Fortunately the horse was not hurt, but these and many other RDA times hold very happy memories for Pam. In 1982 Pam won the Silver Year Cup for most progress at Cobbes Meadow and also came second at the Hever dressage competition. Riding with the RDA has given Pam a whole new outlook on life. After having been totally wrapped up in Highland dancing, suddenly with immobility and frequent surgery to endure, she felt there was no outlet for her emotions. With Cobbes Meadow she has found companionship, exercise, a new fitness and lots to laugh about. Now, having obtained Bronze Award, the next step must be Silver, which is going to involve a lot of hard work but in which Pam is determined to succeed.

Charles and I, and another rider called Dee, felt we would like to continue our exams a little more seriously, and study for our Bronze

Award. We knew this would mean learning a lot more from our books, and we would need to devote more time to stable management and grooming. We were sad at this time to say farewell to Lynne, our treasured instructor, who had helped us all so much, so safely, and with such encouragement and warmth. Lynne had a handicapped daughter and now needed to work and devote more time to her. Anthea volunteered bravely to step in for Lynne, and, although not an instructor, she was happy to take the rides and teach us all she could for our exams.

Each week now we concentrated on developing our riding skills, especially in applying the correct aids, and performing various dressage tests. It was at this time I began to feel less well, and sometimes riding made me very tired. Occasionally having ridden quite strenuously, my legs would begin to shake uncontrollably, with the 'shakes' as I called them, there would be a tense, tight feeling, and some pain, though fortunately not too much for me to cope with. One week the shakes refused to go away even when I dismounted, and Nora our physiotherapist massaged the tired muscles until they returned to normal. Although I could still drive the car, it was becoming more difficult, particularly after riding. Once, on returning home, I parked and feeling very pleased with myself, I almost leapt out of the car, only to fall flat and land up with a very painful knee and lots of bruises.

It was important for Pam, Charles and me to learn as much as possible each week now. I can remember Anthea bringing out a grooming kit, and laying it all out on the ground in front of us. My mind went back all those years when I had so irresponsibly groomed Lucky, not having any idea what I was doing. Now we had to study carefully the name of each item, and how to use it. The brushes all looked alike to me, Anthea showed us the dandy brush, used for removing dirt, but to be used gently, not on the head, mane or tail. It looked like the body brush, but this was for brushing off dust and grease, and for massaging the skin. So it was dandy for dirt, and body for beauty – then the Water brush, shallower in style, to be used to damp the mane, tail and feet. The strange looking curry comb for brushing out the body brush, and only to be used on the horse if using a rubber curry comb on thick dried mud.

The hoof pick was easy to remember, but when we looked at a hoof, there was the frog to learn about, the cleft of frog, and to understand the importance of picking out correctly from the heel towards the toe so as not to damage the sensitive structure of the frog. Two sponges for cleaning eyes and dock seemed like common sense, plus the bucket of water. The stable rubber was for that final shine and, just to impress the examiner, there was also a sweat scraper, a wisp for massage and a tin of hoof oils! So that's what it's all for I thought, and to think I'd groomed Lucky entirely with a dandy brush! We went over the grooming kit several times, testing each other on the correct names and uses of all the items. It was good to be learning properly, and now was an opportunity to put it all into practice. Cassy, a large grey horse stood patiently as we tried to groom him. The problem for all of us was one of balance, sweeping our hand round in a circular direction with the body brush was fine, until one felt oneself gently sweeping towards the ground as balance went astray again! Getting arms up high enough to brush the head gently, or lay the mane, was also a problem but we took it all in good part and spent a lot of time laughing at our feeble efforts. Coaxing Cassy to lift her hoof was a work of art, and bending or squatting while picking out the hoofs was impossible. As it is dangerous to sit on the ground so near to a horse, we had to agree simply to watch this being done by Pauline, Anthea's groom – a super girl who helped us a great deal over the weeks while learning stable management. Eventually Cassy looked extra clean and gleaming, and we prided ourselves on our handiwork.

One week we heard that our Cobbes Meadow group was to raise enough money to build our own new indoor riding school in the grounds of a local hospital at Chartham. Under a committee headed by a local businessman, Alex Bennett, a team would work together to fund raise £50,000, initially and Catherine was to be secretary. It all seemed incredible to me that people could be so dedicated and committed to a project, to give so selflessly of their time and energies to achieve such a goal. I had no doubts that the new school would come about. At present we were generously allowed to ride on one day a week at this riding school in Waltham, but obviously, to have our own school just for RDA would mean we could vastly extend the number of disabled riders who could benefit, and the school would be used each day.

For us as riders, however, our ambitions remained a little more modest, and we set our hearts on obtaining our Bronze Awards and Pam her Silver. We were learning a lot now, and would spend time on getting a good active walk, or an even slow trot, having maximum control over our horses. Another new horse joined us now, this was Polly. Polly Flinders was a dark bay thoroughbred mare 15.3 hands. She had competed in all pony club and riding club activities and had won a great deal. She had competed in BHS one-day and two-day events, and was upgraded to an Intermediate Eventer. She was a little more temperamental than Sherry, and had to be handled carefully, but with the right rider she was obliging and forward-going.

Polly was very sensitive and needed the lightest of handling, and we felt privileged to ride her. I remember one week I had been asked to canter, and this I asked for on the next bend. Polly cantered but felt all wrong – and Lynne, who had returned to give us a special extra bit of coaching, quickly called me back to trot. I couldn't think what was wrong, but then Lynne explained I was on the wrong leg – something I didn't understand at all but was to learn about much later. After our ride that week we had our first attempt at learning something about the tack. We thoroughly examined a saddle, taking time to feel every bump and flap, and slowly to go over the correct names for each part. We also talked about how to hold, clean and store a saddle, as well of course, how to put a saddle on – first on the withers, then eased back into position, and fixed by the girth. The bridle seemed so complicated, and I winced at my past memories of tacking up Lucky! Now we learned how to fit a bridle, but fortunately not too much detail was required for bronze-award, that would come later!

It was a bright sunny day in June, and we were to meet at Womenswold, on a beautiful estate belonging to Caroline, our new secretary. We were to have a dressage competition. Maurice came with me to this event and, enjoying the freedom of a warm day off, we parked our car and ambled over towards the others, now grouped around some horse-boxes and Land Rovers. Sherry was already being warmed up by Charles, and Maurice and I chatted to Peter and Sheila. We were competing in quite a difficult dressage test, and there was much teasing and laughter as we nervously awaited our turn. Maurice had brought a camera with him to snap that special moment! Sherry was in good form – not too fresh, and soon it was Charles' turn to enter the dressage ring. He was riding very well today, and managed Sherry beautifully. He looked so poised, you could hardly believe he had to walk with two sticks. Everyone applauded as he rode out of the ring after his test. It was my turn next, and I chose to ride Sherry who was so responsive, yet calm. Jenny and Catherine helped me mount – in other words, they gave me an almighty shove up, and there I was, all set to go. I felt nervous, and very hot – by now the sun was high in the sky and it beat down on the dry grass from a clear vivid blue sky. I walked around for a few minutes and then the sound of the judges car horn told me it was time to begin. A steady walk in at 'A' up to 'X', halt, salute (and smile at) the judges. Next into the dressage routine I had done my utmost to learn. Round, across the ring at 'F', trot on and canter at 'M', all seemed to be going quite well, then, trotting at a good pace slightly downhill, Sherry slipped on the hot dry grass, her fore legs buckled under her, she went down, and, needless to say, so did I! On the one prestigious occasion that Maurice had brought the camera, there I was performing a most unladylike fall over Sherry's head. Bump – I sat there in the field wondering quite what had happened. Sherry was now standing beside me with a bemused look on her face! Jenny and Anthea ran out to see if I was all right – which I was – my only hurt being my pride and my rear end! I asked to mount again immediately, for although I felt a bit shaken, I was sure it was best to get straight back on board, and carry on! The judges had indicated that I could begin the whole test again, so, with a few extra bruises and shakes, Sherry and I set forth once more into the dressage ring! I don't think we performed all that well the second time, but I felt really pleased we had both coped with our embarrassing fall. A special cheer surrounded us as we finally left the ring – and I felt heartened – and relieved Maurice had not caught that spectacular moment on camera!

We picnicked together, sitting quietly on rugs on the warm grass. It was good to be with so many friends all enjoying a beautiful day. There was time for a short trek around the estate. I rode a young palamino, I'd never seen before. He was very slim, and sensitive, and had a very springy movement with short, exact strides. We trotted under the spreading arches of old English oak trees, and across open land tufted with dried grasses. On our return we watered the ponies and then prepared for prize-giving. Charles had won the dressage, and we were all delighted he had done so well. Pam had also done well, beating me by a few points. Stephen, Peter and Dee also won rosettes, and then the Silver Cup was awarded (for progress during the year) to Peter and me! We were joint winners and were both thrilled-to-bits. It had been a lovely day, and we felt full of gratitude to the helpers who take the time and bother to give us such a happy time, and who make that special effort to catch, groom and tack up their horses for us, let alone bring them miles in horse boxes through the Kent countryside!

The time for the move to Chartham and the new riding school was drawing closer, and there was much excitement as we heard of the very

. . . different types of ponies and their uses learned.

latest progress. By now the work had begun, footings were in, fencing up, and the basic construction was under way. For the time being though Pam, Charles, Dee and I had to study more for the Bronze and Silver Awards. Bedding, feeding, and watering had to be understood and the different types of ponies and their uses learned. Bedding seemed complicated as there were so many different methods. It is hard to understand fully the difference between wheat straw, oat straw and barley straw, when you haven't seen the various types. Peat moss was good especially if there was a fire risk, and wood shavings or sawdust could be used. Alternatively there was the Combination or Deep Litter System. I found it helpful simply to ask horse owners in the area what they used, that gave a more realistic picture of bedding. Trying to learn the various types of foods and their nutrient values was fun. We would inevitably get them all mixed up. We realised with astonishment that none of us had actually seen horses feeding, apart from taking hay from a hay net. Anthea would bring the various types of foods in jars, and we would spend time feeling the oats, barley and nuts, or was it crushed barley or rolled oats? So the learning continued, and slowly we became more familiar with the general care of a horse.

I found it most interesting looking at the various types of horse and pony. We needed to recognise a hunter, a lady's hack, and a cob. Sherry and Polly were both hunters, and Cassy was a cob. There was also the event horse – generally good at most things, and the speedy Arab. The show pony and leading rein pony, and the typical RDA horse – well mannered but responsive, not too wide, not excitable, good with other horses and reliable at all times. I thought back to the ponies I had ridden, to dear old Farthing, all those years ago, who I should imagine was a little Shetland pony. Lucky, probably a cob with her placid temperament and small but stocky build. Then the fabulous little fell ponies in the Yorkshire dales. I had been fortunate to ride such different horses, and hoped now I could remember the names given to their different types.

I was having a little more difficulty in getting around now, and was having to resort more to my wheelchair, which I found most frustrating. The problem wasn't so much the wheelchair, as the fact that someone had to push it as my arms weren't strong enough to manage it myself. I'm an independent person, and I disliked having to depend on others to get around. I could still drive the car, but if Maurice was out or away, I was stuck at home, unable to even get to the village shop or to friends, or to church. In view of this, I made enquiries about having a powered wheelchair. One day a gentleman from a nearby firm came with a powered chair in his van, and showed me how to try it out. The chair was marvellous, moving quietly forward or backward or sideways in response to a little knob you pushed in whichever direction you wished to go. The further you pushed the knob, the faster it went, up to four miles an hour. The chair would climb five-inch kerbs, cope easily with one-in-four hills, and would go twenty-eight miles before it required recharging, which simply meant plugging the chair lead into an electrical socket. I was most impressed especially with its flashing orange hazard lights, indicator lights and horn! Maurice and I both felt the chair would be a great asset in giving me more freedom and in keeping my independence. The new chair arrived within three weeks, and was the beginning of a lot of fun and freedom for me. I could now take the chair to the shop, or into the village to have coffee with friends. I could go for country walks with the family, the chair coping easily with fields, or tracks, and even rough uneven ground. Far from feeling depressed about the chair, I felt very thankful to be able to have it.

Autumn time was with us again, and this year the colours of the trees were dramatically splendid. Browns, reds, oranges and yellows jostled for pride of place in the fields and woodlands. Bright berries heralded a hard winter, and as birds migrated, squirrels busily hid nuts and hedgehogs discovered dry beds of leaves in which to sleep for the winter months. One last treat came nearer for us at Cobbes Meadow, it was to be a trip up to Olympia in London to watch the Christmas Show. Maurice drove me to Canterbury where our coach was to pick us up. Pam and I sat next to each other, and I must confess, we talked all the way to London! At last we arrived at Olympia, and riders and helpers piled out of the coach, wheelchairs were unloaded from the back, and off we set, an odd looking crew to anyone who didn't know who we were. We were fortunate to have a special box which could accommodate the wheelchairs. I sat with Stephen and we thoroughly enjoyed ourselves as we watched the various displays by horses and riders. The memory of the general atmosphere will stay with me a long time – that of colour, music, movement and horses. It was a tremendous experience, and something I wouldn't have made the effort to go to had it not been for Cobbes Meadow arranging everything so beautifully. My feelings of thanks were very deep towards those super helpers who give up so much time so cheerfully to help us to enjoy life. It wasn't just the time, or the effort that they gave, it was that special part of themselves, of their personalities that made being with the RDA such a fulfilling and creative experience of team spirit and trust.

A magnificent Christmas buffet lunch at Jenny's home rounded off the year for us all at Cobbes Meadow. It had been a marvellous year of learning and enjoyment, and we looked forward to even greater things to come in the new year.

Chapter Five

PRINCESS ANNE

Along the north downs there is a beautiful valley sweeping round from Chilham, Garlinge and Petham. To the east lies a high ridge of open land, beyond which spreads the City of Canterbury, its magnificent cathedral rising up like a sacred monument in a mantle of honey-coloured stone. To the west, farmland extends for miles, and to the south, the valley runs up to Old Wives Lees and other villages tucked in amongst the orchards and oast houses. At the centre of this is the village of Chartham with its dominant church tower. Beyond the village, high on the downs, was the psychiatric hospital of St. Augustine, set in extensive grounds. It is here, high on a ridge, that our new school for Cobbes Meadow was built. Driving through the hospital grounds, leaving the main buildings behind, the roadway leads on past an open green field, and there in front is the new large blue indoor riding school. The gate boasts the name of Cobbes Meadow RDA and an expansive courtyard of pressed stones, edged with young fir trees, lies in front of the building. The views stretch on for mile after mile of undulating country, some grazing land, woodland, hills and valleys, and little clusters of homes on hillsides, or oasts set in extensive orchards. The air is clean and sweet, and ridges of cloud can be seen playing shadows across the valleys as the wind blows them on towards the sea. Huge double doors open up to show the inside of the school, the light from the doors flooding in to show the high ridged roof and rustic wood shavings on the floor. Leading off from the main school is a large meeting area or annexe with tack room, stable and toilets. A great thrill of pride goes through me when I think of the tremendous effort made by Jenny and her team, and I think of the generosity of the people of Kent, and further afield, who have given so willingly to make this dream become a reality. As riders

49

we could never really express our thanks and appreciation, but for most, to enjoy the riding and to benefit from it, was thanks enough, and for others of us, the added incentive to pass our exams and win awards for Cobbes Meadow urged us onward.

The Bronze Award exam was now fixed for a day in March. Pam was to take the Silver Award at the same time. As building was still in progress at the new school the exams would be held at Catherine's home where there were stables and all the equipment we might need. Arriving at Catherine's, I have to confess to feeling exceptionally nervous, but before too long, a pleasant looking examiner was striding towards us, hand extended and a welcoming smile on his face. So this was the examiner who was to question us. We sat in our wheelchairs around the stable door, and he let fly a barrage of questions. How would we look after this horse? What type of bedding would we use, and why? What were the various pieces of tack called, how were they cleaned and how should you fit a bridle? The questions flowed on, and the examiner seemed to be enjoying himself. Charles, Dee and I falteringly gave him the answers we hoped he would approve of, and occasionally looked to each other for support or inspiration. What types of horses did we know about and what did we mean by a lady's hack? At last the examiner seemed satisfied with our answers and we set off back to the riding school to demonstrate our riding skills. Dee and I rode Sherry in turn, and Charles rode the cob. Our examiner asked us to walk, trot, sitting and rising, and canter. We had to trot twenty and ten-metre circles, and halt square. We rode serpentine shapes down the school, and also had to show we could rein back. After what seemed ages, the examiner told us we had passed our Bronze Award, and warmly congratulated us. He had been very strict and firm, but I felt I could trust him. He was rather awe-inspiring with his booming voice and penetrating eyes, but a friendly smile belied a tender heart and I felt safe with him and learned to respect him. It was good to hear that Pam had passed her Silver Award, so we were all thrilled and thanked the examiner and Anthea, who had done so much to encourage and teach us. Our next goal now became clear to us – for Charles and me it was the Silver Award, Dee would wait a while before more exams, and Pam would try for Gold.

The marvellous advantage of the new school at Cobbes Meadow was the number of groups of different riders who could be catered for. Monday sees children riding who are physically or mentally handicapped.

Tuesday our advanced group rides. Thursday more children and some severely disabled adults ride. Friday the driving group drives at the school. It is this last group I recently visited.

The driving section of the Riding for the Disabled Association has carefully trained and chosen ponies that have to pass a suitability test. These ponies are put to carriages that are especially made to carry a wheelchair. The wheelchairs are clamped into position to prevent any possibility of movement or rocking. The carriage is made with a special low entrance for the semi-ambulant drivers or 'whips' as they are called. There are strong hand grips and support rails, seats often being fitted with special support cushions.

Competent teaching in the correct style of driving is given by an able-bodied companion whip. There are dual reins to help with driving, only when necessary. Sometimes the whips' disabilities may prevent driving in the orthodox manner, and it is here that ingenious aids are used such as hand holds on the reins, voice substitutes, sounds for the blind to drive to and hand signals for the deaf.

Helpers on the ground are always available with safe and pleasant venues to help to make this exciting sport very safe without taking any of the fun away from it. There are competitions with other disabled whips, and a series of competence tests, leading up to being placed in open competitions. Apart from these, there is the simple enjoyment of driving through the countryside.

The Driving Group of Cobbes Meadow began in 1984. A lady called Joy, who lives locally, had been driving for many years, and now taught Rosemary and Jacky, two RDA. helpers all about driving, so that Cobbes Meadow could have its own group. They attended lectures and demonstrations and eventually they were passed by the RDA. driving committee, fortunately just in time for the opening of the school by Princess Anne – during which they gave their first demonstration. I went up to the riding school one bright, cool sunny day to watch some driving, and to see for myself what the group got up to. When I arrived, whips were being brought into the school annexe in their wheelchairs, and some walked on crutches. It was good to see Stephen there, thoroughly at home amongst the driving group. Two delightful iron-grey Welsh ponies stood patiently by, as they were harnessed up by whips and helpers. Correct harnessing is of vital importance for safety and is part of the skill of driving. I watched with interest as this was taught. Two of the ponies were called Mai and Joci – and they had been working as a pair for over a year.

They compete at local club level in cross country driving, and do very well. Many helpers are needed for the driving group, and each disabled whip must have an able-bodied helper as companion whip. The reins ensure dual control drive when necessary. The disabilities of the whips tends to be more severe than for most RDA riders, and I saw double amputees, severe stroke victims, and serious multiple sclerosis folk thoroughly enjoying themselves as they skilfully manoeuvred the pony carriages. In winter, when it is too cold to drive, the group meet in each other's homes and watch driving videos. The whips take RDA and British Driving Society tests, and soon gain an all-round knowledge of driving. People who are severely disabled are not able to get out into the country, but with pony and carriage, it is possible to drive out through bluebell woods, feel the warmth of the sun and look for primroses. It gives the disabled driver a sense of control and achievement, and they can feel confident in their ability to drive and to enjoy themselves. The pony carriages are especially designed for disabled whips so that wheelchairs can be put straight into the carriage. The design has won awards, and funds from the BDS charity bought the first pony carriage for Cobbes Meadow.

One of the whips who is always at the driving group is Barbara, who has suffered from multiple sclerosis for many years, and is now completely dependent on her wheelchair. She wrote to Hazel, the chairman of the driving group, about how she feels about it all. Here is her letter.

On Fridays we drive with ponies and traps that is, at the Cobbes Meadow Driving Group at Chartham, part of the R.D.A. We have such splendid times: in fact it has added a new dimension to our lives. Where else could we disabled folk find sets of four such strong and willing legs, whose pleasure is to serve us? And with such graciousness and style too? Wheelchairs are right handy, but cuddly they are not! Neither will they work with such zest for a 'Good boy', a pat and a couple of sugar lumps.

We are a very happy group and we 'old' and 'new' hands and helpers have many a laugh. Our helpers are wonderful and do everything they can to give us an enjoyable time. We take great pleasure in each other's achievements and successes. I know my health and spirits have improved as a result.

We have all made good progress, passing Grades I and II of our proficiency tests, and our programme is varied and full. We now have several public appearances to our credit. Steven and I drove at the Malling Show, Sandy and Steven at Windsor, and Ken, as a disabled ex-serviceman represented his regiment by driving in the Lord Mayor's Show.

In winter we meet for videos and talks, and visit such places as the Woods Workshop, where new carriages are built and authentic ones renovated.

This session is now in full swing and the calendar filling up with events. Dressage shows at Malling and Ascot get us off to a flying start and we look forward to more beautiful drives in the countryside.

I don't know if there are ponies and horses in heaven (but personally I think they are much too lovely to be missed out) but all I can say is that when I'm in my pony and trap it's a bit of heaven right here and now.

I sat down on the fresh grass outside the school and watched the driving. The sweet smell of an early May day mingled with the scent of ponies and crushed grass. The soft thud of pony hooves pounding the grass and the whir of wheels gave a precise rhythm, and blended with the chink and clink of harnesses and carriage. The whips' voices would gently instruct the ponies 'walk on', 'trot on' or 'right', and 'halt'. The dressage formations have to be exact and accurate, as in riding; there is no room for carelessness. The change of pace must be noticed and the pony praised and encouraged. To see such disabled people in command was rewarding enough, but the look of pleasure and delight on their faces was the joy of that morning in the sun. One of the whips is called Sandy, and after her drive, she came and chatted to me.

Sandy had been driving with Cobbes Meadow for just a year, and had benefited enormously from it. Sandy told me how she was born in London in 1944. She was a normal baby until at just eighteen months her joints began to swell, and she developed rashes. Within a year she was unable to walk. She was admitted to hospital and remained there from the age of two and a half to six years. The diagnosis was Stills Disease, a type of childhood arthritis, and doctors said she would never walk again. All kinds of treatments were tried, but nothing was able to take away the

The thud of hooves blended with the click of harness and carriage.

constant pain which Sandy was fast becoming used to. Fortunately Sandy was not to be beaten, and having a naturally happy disposition, enjoyed being with other patients and nurses. In those days hospital visiting was very restricted, and Sandy was only able to see her parents just once a month. By the time she was discharged from hospital at six years old, she didn't know her parents. Sandy then attended a special school for the physically handicapped, but although she worked hard, she became very behind in her studies, having missed so much, and by the time she went to a normal school at age eleven, she was far behind in her work. However, pain and immobility had created a fighting instinct in Sandy and she fought not only to catch up at school, but also to walk again. She loved art, especially anything which allowed her to express her creative side, like model making. She was fond of animals and the family kept dogs. She got on well with other children and wasn't deterred when friends affectionately called her 'Peg Leg'.

Over the teenage years Sandy coped with flare-ups in her illness, and periods when she was better and could walk, although with difficulty, and always with pain. At times she chose not to bother, to pretend she couldn't do something to save the effort of trying, but generally she stayed well, with the help of the anti-inflammatory drug Cortisone. When Sandy was fifteen years old her knees became very swollen and painful, and an operation was performed followed by three months of traction in hospital. Eventually Sandy left school and obtained a job as a typist, but she intensely disliked the job, as her ambition was to work with people. When she was nineteen, Sandy left home and stayed in a Church Army Hostel. Further surgery on a painful swollen hip was carried out when Sandy was twenty-one, but the operation was not successful, and Sandy was left with great pain and immobility. She felt miserable and depressed.

Another operation was performed, this time a total hip replacement, and, after seven months in hospital, it was realised the operation had been successful. At last Sandy felt good, and it gave her a new lease of life. Her fighting spirit came to the fore once more and, still having Cortisone to control pain in her knees, she applied to train as a social worker. It was questioned whether she could possibly cope with the hectic pace of the training, as Sandy needed crutches to get around, but undeterred she persisted with the training, and qualified when she was twenty-nine. At last now she could have her wish fulfilled and could work with people. She began working with deaf children, then went on to help cancer patients, as well as working in a psychiatric hospital and running group therapy sessions and helping with marriage counselling. She coped wonderfully with her handicap, although she was never without pain.

Six years ago Sandy met a young priest, Nigel, and soon they were married. However times became hard once more as Sandy became ill again. This time the Cortisone didn't help, and in pain and despair, Sandy was practically bedridden. Once more luck came Sandy's way and she came under a new consultant who started her on a new drug. The months of pain continued, but then after nine months the illness stopped getting worse, and Sandy began once again to get around on crutches. However, she felt lonely and depressed although her worst symptoms had abated. In March she heard about Riding for the Disabled, and set about making enquiries. She phoned Jenny and, not feeling she could cope with riding, was thrilled to hear there was a driving group at Chartham. Sandy had spent several months feeling lonely, lacking in self-confidence, and not going out with friends. Now she had the opportunity to change all that. She began driving with Cobbes Meadow, and immediately felt the stimulus it presented to succeed in doing something physical. Her muscles would ache with tiredness, but she knew that as the weeks went by her muscles improved. She had discovered a new confidence, new friends, and was far more lively. She could walk further, and had even bought a dog which she trained herself. Sandy really enjoyed driving, and had also joined the local Harness Club. After driving for just three months Sandy came in second place at the Windsor British Driving Society show. She passed her Blue and Red felt RDA tests, and hoped to take further British Driving Society tests. Sadly, Sandy died a few years later.

Throughout the Spring of 1984 final preparations were being made to the school. We wondered if everything would be finished in time, and there were last minute hold-ups and panics – but everyone who could, helped in some way – my task being to paint the white letter boards for the dressage ring! Then the great day arrived, it was Monday 14th May 1984 and the day for the official opening of our new riding school by Her Royal Highness Princess Anne had finally arrived.

I had woken early that day and, amongst the excited chatter from the boys, dressed in jodhpurs and white shirt and RDA sweater. We were to be at the school by ten o'clock. We drove up to the hospital grounds, and discovered a huge car park which had been created specially for the occasion. Maurice pushed me in my wheelchair from the car park to the school as it was too far to walk easily, and I would need my chair during the morning. The day was bright and clear, with a chilly wind blowing off the downs. We soon met up with Charles and Pam, and Peter and Sheila, Stephen and others. All the helpers were there and lots of important looking people we'd never seen before! The Princess was to arrive by helicopter, and sure enough, at 10.30 a.m. the whir of helicopter blades could be heard high in the sky, and before we knew it, the gleaming red helicopter landed on the adjacent green. Out stepped the Princess, who was welcomed by a Deputy Lieutenant of Kent. The Princess was then driven by pony and trap to the school by Rosemarie who was in charge of the driving group. It was a marvellous sight, Rosemarie in her green RDA driving sweatshirt, and the Princess wearing a cream-coloured, wide-brimmed hat, and cream short jacket over a rust and brown dress. The Princess waved and smiled as little Midas, the pony, trotted along pulling the trap.

On arrival at the school Princess Anne was welcomed by the Mayor, and was presented with a bouquet of flowers by a lovely little girl called Ursula. Several people were now introduced to the Princess, but we were especially happy to see Jenny and Catherine introduced. We were now mounted, and quietly lined up at the back of the school. I was riding Polly, and as she was so sensitive, I must admit I felt quite nervous, anxious that the crowd of people might upset her. The Princess was now given scissors by young Catherine from the children's group, and proceeded to cut the white tape which was stretched across the school. I could only think of all the tremendous work by so many good people that the tape symbolised. The Princess was now introduced to the Trustees, which included Lynne, our chief instructor and of whom we are all so fond. There followed a simple but moving blessing of the new riding school, performed by the Dean Emeritus of the Cathedral, who was greatly loved by the people of Canterbury.

Now for our big moment. Our group consisted of Pam, Charles, myself, Peter, Stephen and Diane, a blind rider who always showed such courage, but who has now left the area. We were to ride in formation to music, showing skills of control, use of aids, and team work. I was leading file, and as already mentioned, I was riding Polly. The music started, and off we set. Round the school, ask for trot up the long side, up the centre – all seemed to be going all right and all the horses and riders were performing well. I had to concentrate hard on keeping in tune with

Polly, not letting her sense my nervous tension – and remembering the formations. I knew if I went wrong, the whole ride would follow and our patron might not be too impressed! Each time I trotted past the spectators' area Polly flattened her ears – she certainly didn't approve but we kept going, now across the school together, and change the rein, canter on round each in turn, and finally all ride up the centre to end facing the Princess, halt and salute and try to smile! The music ended, the Princess and the spectators applauded, and Jenny looked relieved and pleased. Now the Princess rose to come and present us with special commemorative rosettes. The press were nearest to Polly and me on the right and it was at this point that dear Polly decided enough was enough. She bowed her head low, and purposely strode back several paces – quite out of our neat line! It caused a minor stir amongst the press men, who obviously considered this an amusing and newsworthy incident! I really didn't know what Polly was going to do next! I managed to halt her, and speaking very gently to her I told her to walk on, using my legs so gently the message was almost imperceptible – she hesitated, then rather reluctantly moved forwards, ending up not quite in line, but near enough!

Princess Anne now came to each of us in turn, accompanied by Jenny and Lynne. She talked quietly to each rider – my heart was in my mouth as she approached me. Jenny introduced me, and suddenly we were speaking to each other! She asked me if I always rode Polly, and did we ride outside the school. I answered as best I could but felt distracted by a little thought in my head that kept thinking, "Gosh you're actually talking to Princess Anne, isn't she lovely and natural and interested!" She asked if I enjoyed riding inside – I said I did, especially dressage and jumping. The Princess paused, then smiled broadly and went on to say how she had been teaching her young son dressage yesterday, and that he wasn't paying attention, and shot right off his horse horizontally! We all laughed, and she handed a rosette to me and we shook hands. I thanked her, and said how riding was a real incentive to keep well. She then passed on to meet Charles and talk to him. After all the riders had been introduced, we led off in single file as the Princess returned to her seat. I was shaking all over by the time we emerged into the courtyard and dismounted, thrilled, relieved and thankful all had gone so well. I gave Polly an extra thank you as she had behaved beautifully, even if that included stepping gracefully backwards away from the spectators! Three other riding groups now gave their demonstrations, including the children and the driving group. We understood later that all the rides had gone well, and the Princess seemed to have been really interested and happy. There followed a break for coffee, and Pam, Charles and I sat in our wheelchairs in the school, and were delighted that the Princess came over to us quite informally and spoke to us. She met several people at this stage who had done so much to support the building of the new school.

After coffee, everyone moved outside, and on towards the open paddock. It was here that Charles proudly presented Princess Anne with a spade so that she could symbolically plant a beech tree to commemorate the occasion. Nearby was a fence dividing the RDA land and the hospital grounds. A few patients had gathered behind this fence to watch the Princess, who walked over to them. I think, for me, the most moving occurrence of the whole visit then took place. Some of the patients, part of the ground team who helped with the gardening, had gathered some bluebells from the nearby woods. A large bunch of floppy-looking bluebells was handed over the fence to Princess Anne, who took them gracefully and smiled full of understanding. I could have wept, somehow they meant so much, alongside formal bouquets, a simple bunch of woodland bluebells given by some psychiatric patients. Wonderfully, it was this moment that was captured on the press men's cameras, and was vividly shown in the local newspapers that week. Everyone broke into spontaneous applause, it was a magnificent ending to the visit. Not long after this the Princess left in the red helicopter. She could be seen waving happily to us all at Cobbes Meadow as the loud whir of the helicopter clapped overhead, and the Princess flew out into the distant sky, leaving us with cheer in our hearts and an almost tearful thank you on our lips to the fabulous Princess who had come to open our school which had been built to give freedom, purpose and enjoyment to so many disabled people. The visit had gone perfectly, thanks to Douglas, Catherine's husband, who had organised the day with a mix of military precision and humour.

We heard now that the date for the Silver Award exam was set. It gave us six months to learn all we needed to know, but it wasn't long in which to develop that horse 'sense' we felt was necessary.

Anthea and Pauline worked as hard as we did. They brought all the different types of rugs which the horses wore. The New Zealand rug was the only one we seemed to know about, worn when the horse was out at grass, made of waterproof canvas, and partly lined with woollen material. It was fixed with a surcingle and leg straps, and provided protection from wind and rain. Straightforward enough, but what of the woollen day-rug? Were they used these days, and is the jute night-rug still practical when horse owners seemed to use washable quilted rugs? Was the sweat sheet used under a rug to keep the horse from overheating, or cooling off too quickly? Some degree of confusion arose, and we spent a lot of time discussing and arguing the merits of one type of rug against the other, and we practised putting on the rugs and applying the rollers or surcingles. We also studied the three main types of clips, and learned when, how and why a blanket clip was used, as against a trace or hunter clip. We were conscious of our knowledge being very theoretical and wished we had more opportunity of seeing or working with horses so that we weren't simply learning from books. However, the morning we met at Catherine's home to study bits was confusion par excellence! Spread out before us were about ten different types of bits and snaffles. We had tremendous fun, as we tried to learn the difference between the eggbutt snaffle and the Fulmer snaffle. The loose ring snaffle seemed to be the same as the Fulmer, but the Kimblewick was different with its 'D' rings, and with its distinctive port, or raised piece on the mouthpiece. Having learned that, we discovered several others had ports, and the difference between the Weymouth and the Pelham still baffles me! Charles was actually very good at learning these, and in his calm way usually got it right. Pam, Dee and I muddled through, and Peter and Stephen did well. Back at the riding school we would minutely study the difference and reasons for using a Cavesson noseband, or a Grackle or Dropped noseband, and how to fit them.

Perhaps the hardest skill we had to acquire now was how to jump. We had for a long time been walking or trotting over poles, but we hadn't actually learned to jump. We started by learning the correct posture for jumping and progressed to jumping over poles about a foot off the ground. The problem was, that although we knew it was only a foot off the ground, Polly liked to think she was jumping at Beechers Brook, and would almost stop, then leap up high, usually managing to throw Pam, Charles or me rather spectacularly into the air. I always had to smile at Charles who would fall with such a thump, we were sure he must have injured himself, but then there was that same old smile as he reached out to put his glasses back on, which had also gone for six along with him! We soon decided not to jump with Polly, but to stay with Sherry who was so good, and gave us all a sense of confidence. We did find jumping difficult, my legs just didn't seem strong enough to cope with the landing, and I had not the necessary balance, added to which, I have to admit that I felt afraid. It was tremendously exciting trotting up to a jump, then just at the vital moment when I should have encouraged Sherry to jump, I would suddenly meet that great wall of fear and imagine I was jumping a six foot fence at Olympia, and hold back, thus confusing Sherry, and frequently landing up on my bottom. We needed to persevere, as for the Silver Award we had to jump over two foot jumps from both trot and canter. I think if I were honest, none of us really enjoyed jumping at this stage. It was only in later months that confidence brought about real enthusiasm for it.

Chapter Six

SILVER LINING

After months of cold wet grey weather; with leaves shivering and daffodils holding back in buds, reluctant to emerge, unexpectedly towards the middle of May, there was a day of real warmth. One could almost hear a sigh of relief as blossoms opened to show off pink and white, and pale green leaves carefully unfurled in quiet offering to the warmth of the sun. On such a day I ventured up to the riding school to meet the children who rode at Cobbes Meadow, and to watch them ride.

The children's groups were organised by Cinders and Anne, both confident, warm people who love the children and who devote so much energy and time to them. On Monday morning Cinders welcomed me and explained about the children's group. There were eight children, aged between four and seven years. All the children were physically handicapped, some had suffered damage at birth, others had congenital problems such as spina bifida, a malformation of the nerves of the spine. They looked a cheerful little group, and the ponies they were to ride looked equally delightful. Little 'Robie', a piebald Shetland pony just 11 hands stood patiently waiting to be tacked up. Nearby stood 'Cola' a beautiful Palamino 12 hands. The children were quietly excited. I watched as Sarah, just seven, on her second visit to Cobbes Meadow, was lifted gently and safely up on to Robie's back. The look of wonder and pride on that little girl's face was long to be remembered as she and Robie calmly walked off, with a helper leading and helpers at each side, securely holding Sarah. After a ten-minute walk, Sarah and Robie tried a little trot together, helpers holding firmly and praising and encouraging both pony and rider. There was a look of thrill and triumph on Sarah's face as she glanced to make sure mum was watching! What an achievement, and what wonderful things to be able to tell her teachers and friends at school who had all been so kind and encouraging. As I watched I realised how vital it was for these children, all of whom had real physical difficulties to cope with in their lives, to feel that they had succeeded and to feel proud of themselves. The riding gave them status as well as an immense pleasure and excitement. Other children were helped to mount ponies, and were led away into the sunshine, their little faces radiant with pleasure. Young Catherine, a pretty little girl with dark hair and large eyes, smiled broadly from under her black riding hat, and called out to her mother to watch her on Tina, a lovely-looking dun pony.

Catherine's mother came over to me and as we sat on the grass in the warm sun she told me how Catherine was their first and only child. The pregnancy had been normal and it was only during labour that difficulties arose. The baby had turned into a poor position and high forceps were needed to rotate Catherine before she could be delivered. After birth Catherine was taken to special care as a precaution and it was there, eight hours following her birth, that little Catherine collapsed. The problem was brain damage following the especially difficult forceps delivery. The baby now showed some paralysis down the left side, affecting her arm and leg. After three anxious days Catherine's parents were told it was most likely that Catherine would die, and that if she did live she could be 'like a vegetable'. They were absolutely shattered and being Catholic, little Catherine was baptized on the third day after her birth, and miraculously she became stronger. She remained in special care in an incubator for sixteen days, then, still with little hope, she was taken home. Now the devoted care and love of Catherine's parents for her showed through, as day after day little Catherine cried. She was put on sedatives and only after four months did the agitation cease and Catherine settled down. For her parents it was a constant battle to save her. They 'tunnelled into her completely', spending all their time stimulating her, holding, touching, loving and talking to her. She looked such an attractive and beautiful baby, her parents just couldn't give up hope. At six months they went to see the paediatrician again. He had sad news for them, for although Catherine seemed to be responding well, her head and brain were not growing, and there was still little hope. Catherine looked well and was the right height. She was responding, smiling and affectionate, and the fact that at a year Catherine could eat on her own was great encouragement for her parents. At two years

Catherine walked and there seemed to be general improvement. Speech soon followed and at two and a half it was noticed that her head, and therefore her brain, was growing normally. She could walk almost perfectly and went to playschool where she proved to be very sociable and happy. She sang songs and played games, but her left arm and hand remained almost useless. The left leg was improving dramatically and little Catherine would walk for miles. She was a secure little girl, and didn't object to leaving mum to go to playschool twice a week and to a special child assessment centre for three days a week. At the age of five, Catherine went to a normal primary school where she did extremely well, although she lagged behind the other children in reading and writing.

Catherine's parents heard about the RDA through the child assessment centre. The children would be taken to RDA at Waltham, and later at Chartham, one day a week. Catherine was terrified at first, and would cry, and not want to get on a pony at all. The helpers were patient and persevered. Eventually Cinders 'plonked' little Catherine on to Robie's back and she began to enjoy the experience and gain confidence. After a time she greatly improved and was now managing a rising trot with a little help. Catherine's mother told me that riding had helped Catherine's co-ordination and given her real confidence. She enjoyed RDA immensely and thrived from the stimulation it offered. Catherine found status in riding and felt it was something she could succeed in: it was young Catherine who presented the scissors to Princess Anne at the official opening of the school, and she herself was presented with a rosette – a great thrill for a very special five year old.

On the same day in the afternoon, I met a different group of children. They came in a minibus from a special school for the severely mentally handicapped. It was a tremendously moving experience as this group of children stood around the field eagerly waiting to mount their special ponies. There were lots and lots of big smiles from under equally big black riding hats, and little eyes that would light up with glee at the sight of a horse. Each child had two or three helpers to themselves. These children were severely brain damaged and some had Downs Syndrome. Young Micky, aged fifteen, was epileptic and had cerebral palsy, and had an abnormally small head. He loved his riding and looked forward to it each week. His teacher told me that he remembered the names of the ponies he rode and that riding was very important to him. The children were sometimes frightened to begin with but the teachers and the RDA helpers found the children especially well behaved when with the horses. It encourages speech for those children who manage to say the pony's name, or to say 'walk on' or 'trot on'. The pleasure on their faces was proof enough of their enjoyment. For some, speech was not possible, and the children needed to touch, feel and smell the horses.

For these children there was a natural affinity between the horse and child. One such child was James, who was aged ten, and cared for in the special care unit for the severely handicapped. Although James had few words, his world was a mixture of sounds, shapes, colours and sensations. In many ways he was shut off in a world of his own, and he was unable to concentrate for more than a few seconds at a time. Yet I saw James' face light up with pleasure as he was gently lifted up on to a pony's back. His hands stretched out along the pony's mane, feeling the coarse hair. The teacher told me how James showed his excitement and pleasure when they were going to riding. He would shake and giggle and try to be first on the minibus! Now as he walked round the field, his face catching the breeze and the sunlight, James turned his head up and around, squinting in the brightness, with a large smile and with sounds of pleasure.

My attention was caught now by another scene. Annie, aged eleven, a Downs Syndrome child, obviously didn't want to ride that day. The helpers led her to her pony, praised her and gently encouraged her to mount, but no, Annie would have none of it, and turned round with her back to Tina, the pony, with arms crossed and mouth firmly shut. Further persuasion was to no avail, until one of the helpers decided that she herself would ride, hoping that Annie would lead her – that's just what happened and little Annie immediately took hold of the leading rein, and proudly strode on ahead, leading Tina and rider round the field! A young boy now tugged at my arm. I asked him if he had ridden and did he enjoy it, he nodded, and said grandly that he had ridden two ponies that day, and he pointed to each in turn, leaving me in no doubt at all of the enormous pleasure and benefit that riding was for these severely damaged children who had such a right to life, its goodness and pleasures.

One Saturday we met together at Anthea's house. The old worn horseshoe clanged loudly as it fell on to the stone yard, the pinchers were laid down. The rasp was held firmly by the farrier as he filed the wall of Sherry's foot ready to fit the new shoe. Our group had all come to study shoeing on this chilly but sunny day, and were watching the farrier about his task of hot-shoeing Sherry. We pulled the travelling rugs Anthea had provided further over our legs. The chill wind competing with the pale sun and the heat of the fire from the forge. The new shoes were glowing red in the fire, and now, with a great searing scorching swirl of smoke, they burnt and singed on Sherry's foot marking how closely the new shoes would fit. Sherry stood patiently, obviously used to the routine, and enjoying the unexpected audience keenly gathered around her. Now the farrier, a bronzed, lined man like a picture from a bygone age, laid the shoe on the anvil, and the sound of metal on metal vibrated through the air as vivid orange sparks sprayed down on to the cold stone. Satisfied with his handiwork, the craftsman lowered the glowing shoe deep into the cold water which made a vicious spluttering hiss.

Knowing the fit was good and close, he took the nails and carefully hammered each nail into the foot, away from the white line, yet firmly up through the hard insensitive wall of the hoof. Three nails on the inside, four on the outer side. Finally he twisted off the ends of the nails emerging through the wall and hammered the nail heads against the hoof and rasped them smooth so the clenches lay flush against the wall. He dropped Sherry's foot from between his legs and stood back, straightening himself as he proudly surveyed his work, wiping the back of his rugged hand over his forehead. We were intrigued by all we had seen and asked many questions. What was the purpose of the frog? What was a pricked foot? Why did the clenches rise when re-shoeing was needed? At last the picture from our text books became a clear reality in front of us as we watched the procedure again on the other foot. Anthea was delighted with our interest and lively participation, and we were only too pleased with the marvellous opportunity to learn all there was to know about shoeing and the structure of the foot. We knew how vitally important it was to understand the foot, as problems with shoeing and the foot are the main cause of lameness in a horse.

As the autumn months came, so we grew anxious to take the Silver Award exam and have the test behind us. Pam, who was now studying hard for gold, and Charles and I, constantly tested each other on various fragments of knowledge we had gleaned from some book, or from our many informative helpers. I wasn't feeling well now, and studying, along with worries over the boys and trying to finish writing a book on childbirth, all took their toll, and I became increasingly tired. At last November bleakly blew into the year, and the ground turned cold and brown as leaves fell and furrowed fields froze. At Cobbes Meadow we repeatedly went over questions and answers, handled tack and revised the points of the horse. Forelock, poll, atlas, mane, followed by crest, withers, croup and dock, we wondered if we would ever remember. Hock, shannon, fetlock, pastern, coronet, so these terms rang round our heads until we nearly said them in our sleep. Dressage was now taken very seriously, and we would practise our trotting and cantering, for ever trying to improve our position and style. For Charles, Pam and me, it was not always easy. Limbs would tire very easily and none of us had correct feelings in our legs; it was hard to know where one's foot was, let alone whether it was giving the correct aid or not and whether the heel was down. However, we persevered and at last the day of our exam arrived and we prepared ourselves for the examiners' onslaught!

It was a grey November day and Cobbes Meadow looked bleak. We shivered with nerves and with cold as we saw the examiners arriving to take our Silver Award and for Pam, her Gold. Very soon we were mounted and, each in turn, demonstrated our dressage and various riding skills. Sherry as usual was in peak form, and seemed to know exactly what we expected of her. Anthea stood by nervously, smiling broad smiles of reassurance. We trotted, cantered and jumped, and hoped desperately our riding was up to standard. There followed the theoretical part of the exam and we gathered around the stable in the annexe in our wheelchairs. The questions followed each other so quickly we hardly had time to breathe between giving our answers. What were the problems associated with shoeing? What was a hunter clip? Describe the various rugs you might use for your horse? Which type of bandaging would you use for travelling, how was it applied? How much oats would a working hunter need per day? By now Charles and I were helping each other by interjecting with the answer if we knew it, and our examiners didn't seem to object. We were both answering well, so far we were covering ground we had thoroughly learned. Eventually the flow of questions ceased, and the examiners left us to go and have a walk together around the school. We knew our fate was being decided at this point. Charles and I felt that if we had failed we didn't honestly feel we could have done more at the time; Pam was feeling pretty low. At last the examiners came to us and asked for Pam to go and join them across the school. After about ten minutes they returned to us. We quickly gathered that Pam had failed Gold, and we felt so sad for her. To our relief, Charles and I were congratulated on passing our Silver Award. We had apparently done well, and our relief was enormous.

However, our jubilations were somewhat dampened as we felt for Pam in her disappointment. Her riding was up to Gold standard, but her theory had let her down. We decided there and then that we would all work for Gold Award together over the following months, and try to take the exam sometime the following year. Relieved and tired, and still cold, we left Cobbes Meadow, another hurdle overcome and yet another hurdle to face; could we ever succeed in gaining our Gold? We felt deeply grateful to Anthea and Jenny, Catherine, Sheila and all the other helpers like Carole, Clare and Liz who were always there to help us and encourage us.

Over the next few weeks we tried to relax and simply enjoy riding for its own sake, with no thought of exams. I felt increasingly tired, and soon suffered a mild relapse of my multiple sclerosis, with my legs becoming limp and numb. I had to stay in bed most of the time, and my doctor insisted on complete rest. Physiotherapy was helpful and gradually, after about six weeks, some strength returned to my legs, and I began to walk again but felt very weak. Did this relapse throw doubt on my ability to take the Gold Award? It was too early to say, all I could do was to get really well again, and keep hoping. Hope was something which helped many of my disabled friends to keep going. Other people go through so much stress that it makes our disabilities shrink before our eyes.

One day Sheila told me about Peter, her second son in a family of four children. The pregnancy had been completely normal, and the delivery although not easy, was without any undue complications. Peter was, at birth, a seemingly normal little boy, and as a baby gave no cause for concern. He was an active, cheerful lad. At the age of two Sheila became concerned that Peter wasn't talking. She took him to see a consultant who made light of the anxiety and said Peter would soon be talking too much! By the age of three, Peter was still not talking at all. Sheila and her husband took Peter to an ear, nose and throat specialist in London and then on to a Harley Street consultant. This doctor diagnosed Peter as being congenitally aphasic, or born without speech. Peter's parents were terribly concerned now. Peter seemed normal in so many ways. He mixed with friends and played well. He was obedient, seemed to understand yet couldn't talk. Unable to get into a special school for speech handicapped children, at five years Peter started at a local primary school. His behaviour was normal in every way in matters such as eating and playing, but he was very poor with reading and writing.

The family believed very strongly that whatever Peter's problem was, he should not be sent away to boarding school, as family love and support came first. Peter was such an attractive looking boy, and friends and family were marvellous in helping in any way they could. Peter made friends wherever he went. As his ability at school was behind his age group, and as his fine co-ordination was poor, it was realised that special teaching was needed for him. By now he was attempting to make sounds. He often successfully said the beginning of a word, but failed to add the end. The first real breakthrough came when Peter went to the Nuffield Centre in London and began working on a structured system of word learning. This continued for three years and led to a marked improvement. When Peter was eleven the family moved to Canterbury and, as there was no suitable school, Peter stayed with his grandmother in Thanet during the week, attending a special school, and returning home each weekend. Peter would play cowboys and indians, and could ride a bike. He could read and write to the ability of a seven year old and had a very good pictorial memory. By the age of sixteen Peter had not progressed very far. He was able to make himself understood by some words and sounds and gestures. He was very aware of all that went on around him, and was emotionally sensitive to situations.

Peter's parents came to realise that if he could work on the land, he could do well, even with his lack of words. They bought a smallholding, and taught Peter to tend the animals, rotavate, cut grass and measure out animal feed. He left school at sixteen and became fully employed on his parents' farm where he worked hard. He had plenty of contact with people as he sold eggs and vegetables and yoghurt. When Peter was twenty-four, Sheila heard about RDA from a friend, and knowing how good Peter was with animals, she felt it could be a help and pleasure for him. Peter's first reaction was very good and under Lynne's excellent instruction, he made good steady progress. He has successfully taken four felt tests, and has now taken, and passed, his Bronze Award – a tremendous achievement. He needs to concentrate very hard to be able to carry out instructions, and he finds it almost impossible to remember the order of things. Simple instructions one at a time, are best. With lots of practice, Peter is able to develop and stick to a routine. He is a good horse rider, competent at a rising trot and canter, and able to jump. His hands are sensitive and he is good with Polly, who needs a careful rider. He has been on five Welsh riding holidays with RDA which he has enormously enjoyed. Peter is very caring, and is helpful with the horses and other riders. Sheila believes that RDA has given Peter terrific confidence. Riding is the first activity he has been successful at, and where he has achieved competitive results. RDA has given Peter friends, and trust. He has enormous confidence in Anthea, and will jump and go on sponsored rides. Sheila feels that RDA is a vital part of Peter's social life, and is of mutual benefit to both riders and helpers.

It is this benefit, this unlimited care and encouragement which came alive when I heard about the special children's holidays organised by Gillian who had been a helper at Cobbes Meadow for many years. I went to discover more, and took one of my boys for a drive out into the countryside. The Plough Inn sign swung gently in the breeze. I stopped the car; an elderly couple were coming slowly down the little village lane, and I asked them where the farm was. Turn right along a very narrow country lane, right at the T-Junction and along another windy lane, and there, across the road, is the farm. I thanked them and drove on, the cow parsley along the tall banks of the lane brushed the sides of the car. This was the depths of the Kent countryside and I was trying to find the farm where Gillian lived.

It was in 1983 that Gillian and Tricia had gone to an RDA teaching day and had visited a farm which ran holidays for disabled children. Gillian soon realised that this was something she could do. Her large old rambling farmhouse was ideal. A stable yard close by, lawns and small pastures, an old open barn and a heated outdoor swimming pool all lent themselves admirably to the concept of holidays for disabled children. Gillian talked to other RDA helpers, to local friends from the village, as well as a local rector, and soon help was offered from all directions. The village friends would organise the cooking for a week, using Gillian's very ample farmhouse kitchen with its Aga and huge wooden table. Other village friends would come each day to help with the children, and to assist the more experienced RDA helpers who would also devote the week to the children. Friends lent their caravans for the children to sleep in and these would be placed near to the house. Two children would sleep in each of the five caravans, so there was no need for bunk beds, which would pose a problem for disabled children, and two nurses would sleep in another caravan, to be on site should there be a problem during the night. So it is that in June of each year, eight physically disabled children come from various RDA groups all over the southern counties, to have a wonderful week's riding holiday with Gillian. The children are aged from ten to fourteen, and have any type of

The reliable little ponies take their precious loads.

physical disability which does not necessitate a wheelchair. Some children have cerebral palsy, some have leukaemia, brain damage following meningitis or some have suffered strokes. The fortunate children are carefully selected by Gillian from lists of children sent by RDA headquarters. It is important that the degree of physical handicap is not so severe that steps are impossible or the child will not really benefit from the facilities that the farm can offer.

Each morning during the holiday week, the children wake early. They are helped to dress by Gillian and the nurses before eight, and go and wash in the house, where they can also bath. A wholesome breakfast is served at eight o'clock, after which the children make their beds and tidy their caravans, with help from the adults. Inspection follows, with much fun and laughter! Once all is ship-shape, the children play games or read or write letters home, while some play French cricket. At nine o'clock the riding helpers arrive. The ponies are already at the farm, and belong to various friends and RDA helpers in the area. Now the real business of the day can begin, each child has two helpers who stay with that child all week. They set about catching and grooming their particular pony, tethered to a long fence. Once the pony is thoroughly groomed, the helpers assist the child to tack up the pony correctly, and then all is ready for the ride With the child proudly mounted, an RDA helper leads, and the helpers stay each side of the pony to give extra safety and security. The children are used to riding with their local groups, but the thrill of riding never goes and these children feel confident and successful as they ride the pony round the field, which is set out as a riding school. After a warm-up, the children go out into the superb country riding down winding lanes, up hills, through narrow gaps in hedges, and even up steep banks; the reliable little ponies carrying their precious loads. The helpers keep the children safe, and enjoy the ride as much as the youngsters, the children may ride for as long as two hours, and become quite tired as they return in time for lunch. They tether and water the ponies together, then go into the kitchen for a tasty lunch round the great wooden table. After lunch there is a quiet restful period, children may draw and colour, write letters or play games.

Each afternoon there is a special visit. The children take a picnic tea and go to visit a dairy, or a pig farm. Sometimes they go to swim and play on a nearby beach, or they might swim at the beautiful heated pool on the farm. One day the children ride their ponies through woodland, and all have a marvellous picnic with the ponies tethered nearby. It is a particular tradition of these holidays that the food is of an excellent standard, and at seven o'clock a delicious supper is served by friends from the village. Following supper, although all are fairly tired by now, there are more games, or a scavenger hunt, a video to watch, or a quieter game of 'wink murder' and one night a barbecue is held at the farm. By nine o'clock, or sometimes a little earlier, the children are really tired and ready for bed, and the helpers settle the children down for a good night's rest.

For some disabled children this week's holiday is their first experience of being away from home. Some of the children have led particularly sheltered lives, and the change of staying in a caravan on a farm is a very valuable experience. Sometimes a child is homesick for the first day or two, but the helpers develop very close loving relationships with the children and help them through the homesick period. It gives a child confidence in themselves to overcome these feelings of sadness at leaving their own home. Through the week there is lots of fun and laughter, hugs and help over a few tears, or a hand to hold on a walk, or a cuddle from Gillian (looked upon as mum for the week) or, another favourite helper. If there is a difficult time when there are a few tears, there are delightful things to do to distract, like going to see the adorable ginger kittens, or playing with the four dogs on the farm, or going to have a quiet hug with a special pony, even sitting quietly making daisy chains can settle a child down. The relationships formed become very deep, and one teenage helper, the rector's daughter, writes to the children and receives letters from them throughout the year.

Altogether the week gives an enormous amount of enjoyment to both helpers and riders. Great friendships are made and for the children it is a broadening out of their lives, which are sometimes very protected because of their disability. The ability to cope with home sickness, to form new friendships and to transfer affections is a point of growth and emotional development for these needy youngsters. It gives them a new freedom and independence; courage to cope with trekking with the ponies, and new insights into country life and beauty.

One little ten year old girl, who only had one arm, wrote to Gillian after her holiday; I think her letter sums it all up:

Dear Gillian,

Thank you for all the thing you dun for us.

I wish I can come again to Kent it is lovely I thing, and thank you very much for letting me ride Troy the pony. She is lovely I thing, if I can come nest year and ride Troy it would be lovely. And the food was so lovely.

I like Anne my helper, she so good to us I thing.

Thank you for all the thing you help me with, lots of love, I love you,

Ricky.

Chapter Seven

JUMPING FOR JOY

One year a very pleasant lady mayor was elected for Canterbury which was to bring further good fortune for Cobbes Meadow. The Mayor chose Riding for the Disabled as her charity for the year and all money raised would go to Cobbes Meadow. We were very grateful to Hazel as we came to know her, and many a time, in spite of a hectic schedule, she was to be seen up at the riding school lending a hand or presenting a cheque. The Mayoress, Hazel's daughter, had a pony which was brought up to the school to help with riding. It was felt that the indoor school would benefit from having a spectators' gallery, and it was to this end that the Mayor's charitable money was given. By the end of the year almost £3,000 had been raised, and work progressed with this further expansion of the school.

Much to our delight, permission had now been granted for our riders to trek through adjacent woodland. It was one clear warm day in May that we ventured out beyond the boundaries of the school field. I was riding Mishy, the skewbald, Charles was on Sherry, Dee on Polly, Peter on Abbey and Stephen on Cob. As we turned into the wood we were stunned by the beauty before us. The sun shone in long shafts through the light green trees, young in foliage. At our feet lay a dense carpet of misty blue as all around and far into the distance spread out before us this sea of blue tranquillity, proud and graceful bluebells bowing their dainty heads. The fragrance from the bluebells was unforgettable, and mixed with the clear spring air and the smell of the horses, it left one with a sense of real elation. It was good to be alive, good to be able to appreciate this beauty, good to be taken by four strong dependable legs deep into the woodland where wheelchairs would have been impossible.

Yes, there are difficulties and depressions for most disabled riders, but experiences such as a ride like this make those difficulties fade away. We gently wound our way along the specially prepared track, carefully guiding our horses round trees and up and down little hollows. Claire was walking ahead of us, and other helpers were close by ready to give any help should it be needed. Emerging from the dappled sun in the woodland, we turned along a fieldside track. The gently undulating countryside reaching out for mile after mile, spreading itself out beneath this first real sun and warmth of the year. Mishy was obviously as thrilled as I was with this outing, and his pace was keen and light as we trotted through the open countryside, his ears forward and his mane dancing in rhythm with his movement. Polly was feeling her freedom, and was a little too fresh, so I took leading file, and Polly settled nicely behind Mishy. Eventually we headed back towards the school, all of us having benefited from that ride, a little tired yet very happy.

One day I talked to Stephen's mother about the difficulties and triumphs of her son's life. He had been born in Suffolk, the third child in the family. It had been a normal pregnancy, but the labour was very quick, and the after-birth was delivered first, then baby Stephen was delivered, rather blue and with a notably high pitched cry. He continued to cry and wouldn't feed. The following morning the midwife called a doctor who took Stephen into hospital where he was placed in an incubator. He was christened and his parents were simply told that he might not live as the doctors thought he was brain-damaged. Four anxious weeks passed, but Stephen pulled through and was sent home. The only information given by the doctors was that Stephen was 'brain damaged to some extent'.

Stephen's family moved to Ireland with the army, and it was there, when Stephen was ten months old, that a health visitor called, and told Stephen's mother that the baby was spastic. She had realised something was wrong with Stephen and had compared his progress with other babies but hadn't any idea what the problem was. The label of Athertoid Spastic was a profound shock. When Stephen was three years old, the family moved to Canterbury. Stephen began a course of physiotherapy, but he was unable to walk or talk, or feed himself, and he required total care throughout each day. A friend suggested that Stephen's mother contact the Spastic Society and, after a letter was written asking for help, a lady visited and was able to discuss the situation and give some reassurance. At this time a doctor saw Stephen and recommended that he should have all his teeth extracted, as they had developed without any enamel and were causing pain. At the same time Stephen developed fits, which, it was felt were linked to the pain from his teeth. At the age of four all Stephen's teeth were removed.

When Stephen was five he went for a week of assessment at a special centre at Bexhill. The conclusion was that Stephen was intelligent enough to benefit from a boarding school education, and after further interviews he was offered a place at the Wilfred Pickles School in Peterborough. Stephen was still unable to walk or talk. He made sounds which nobody except his mother understood. A spastic tongue and no teeth made speech impossible. By eleven years Stephen had clearly shown he was a bright boy with a mind of his own. He had the opportunity now of adopting a wheelchair as his mode of getting about, but Stephen flatly refused! One day a teacher told him to go and get some paper, and to his amazement Stephen stood up in his jerky and unco-ordinated way, and walked over to get the paper! Such is his determination to cope with his enormous difficulties. Stephen now changed schools and went to a special boarding school at Tonbridge, where he stayed until he was seventeen. Over his teenage years Stephen had continued to develop his walking ability, and he tried hard with speech, though this was not clear and his spastic movements made his limbs continually move beyond his control.

Once Stephen left school there was nowhere in Canterbury for him to go. Eventually a place was offered at a sheltered workshop for the mentally handicapped, and reluctantly Stephen attended there for three years. He worked in the garden but he found the lack of conversation and communication terrible. He hated this experience and felt depressed and frustrated. His condition worsened both emotionally and physically. Sensing further problems, Stephen's mother managed to stop full time work and took on part time employment, thus freeing herself to look after Stephen at home. He left the workshop and began work as a clerk at the centre for the disabled in Canterbury. The centre runs a helpline called *Dial*, or Disabled Information and Advice Line, and Stephen works with a partner who speaks to the callers while Stephen finds all the right forms and information relevant to the call.

One good thing that arose from his time at the workshop was Stephen's introduction to Riding for the Disabled. He was taken to Waltham each week and, although initially frightened of riding, Stephen was naturally fond of the horses and under Lynne's careful instruction he made steady progress, and he began to develop a new confidence in himself and in his ability to ride. Stephen made new friends, and learned to trust helpers and instructors – above all, he really enjoyed himself.

Stephen now leads quite a busy life. Monday sees him at *Dial*, Tuesday he rides with us at Chartham, Thursday he goes to a woodwork group and on Friday Stephen joins the RDA Driving Group – and there's a twice weekly visit to the local pub for a pint! I asked Stephen's mother what she felt RDA had done for Stephen, and she immediately replied, "Given him strength of character and strength physically. His walking has improved and he enjoys riding so much." I think all credit goes to R.D.A. and to Stephen for being so courageous. He has taken and passed all his felt exams, and last year Stephen amazed us all and won our admiration as he gained his Bronze Award. One gets the feeling with Stephen that, as he wins friends, he will continue to win his way over many hurdles.

Our Gold Award exam was now only six weeks away and Pam, Charles and I were becoming distinctly apprehensive. Jumping was a special cause for concern. We had all had our falls whilst jumping, and consequently there was quite a high degree of anxiety. I felt I could jump providing I could overcome this sudden fear that came over me just as I should be letting the horse jump. One Tuesday morning a special instructor came. She had been a chief instructor for the Pony Club and now she could assess my riding and my physical capabilities. We went into the indoor school where a course of jumps had been put up. The instructor first asked me to walk round, making the correct jumping movements as I did. Having improved on the basic posture, I commenced trotting over very low poles. I still felt very unsteady particularly on landing. Higher poles were provided, and I felt more secure, beginning to sense the horse's keenness to jump and how I must not hold back at the last moment. I was now asked to jump at the canter over a jump no more than two foot high. This was exactly the situation I dreaded. I was afraid Sherry would get excited and jump far too high if I encouraged her. However, our special instructor had gained my confidence, and I asked Sherry to canter as we approached the jump, then just before jumping I asked her to jump, leant forward, allowed with the reins, and over we went with a smooth landing the other side. It had felt quite different from anything I had done before. I felt triumphant. We talked about how I had prepared for the jump, and why it had been successful. I was asked to try another, followed by a double jump. A steady canter, ask for jump, bend forward and again a good landing, then time for the next jump, forward, up, and down, and yet another jump, and I felt as if I'd jumped at Olympia! My legs were shaking and felt quite out of control. I'd done enough, but was thrilled this instructor had really broken down that wall of fear I had experienced before. I was actually enjoying jumping.

I discovered now that my legs often became very shaky, not only when riding, but also when driving the car. My doctor told me very kindly, but quite definitely that he would only allow me to drive if I changed to a fully automatic car especially adapted for hand controls. This was a real blow as I felt one step closer to becoming unable to drive at all. However, we managed to purchase an automatic car, and I arranged for a man to come and adapt it. I lectured myself sternly on how fortunate I was to be able to drive, and how sensible my doctor was, and tried to be positive about it all. I must admit I found it hard to accept and it took a long time to feel confident driving with hand controls.

The pressure to study for the Gold Award was really on now. I spent hours studying horse manuals, learning every fact I could find, but I still felt it was all theory. To try to put the balance right, I asked Catherine at what time she first went out to her horses in the morning. I asked if I could come and watch her, so it was that at seven o'clock one morning I was greeted by an amused Catherine, who proceeded to explain exactly what she was doing, and what foods and amounts of food she was giving to her horses. It all began to feel more real. I began to ask various other horse owners what and when and how they fed and cared for their horses. I visited other friends and watched feeding, mucking out and tacking up. I was interested in the variety of ways in which horses were fed, depending on the work the horse was doing, and the fads or wishes of the owners. Some gave oats, others felt that oats made their horse too hot, some fed pre-mixed food such as oats, barley, nuts and bran. I was trying to convert the text book theory into a kind of horse-sense. I needed to live and work with horses for some time, but as this was impossible I gleaned all I could from many sources. I bought all the current copies of horse magazines and read them avidly. This was a help, and I even learned a lot from the advertisements – little tips like what to use on wounds such as Animalintex for poultice dressings and various other bits of information!

Charles and I had a good morning's revision down at Anthea's. We discussed the management of the horse throughout the year, when to shoe, clip, and prepare for the hunting season. How to adjust feeding to the work asked of the horse. Anthea made me laugh – she would tell us to say to the examiner, "I would call my farrier", rather than simply ask to get the horse shod! We went over and over the most common ailments in a horse, and how to treat them. I counted twelve diseases of the foot alone and became quite amused at trying to sort out the differences between Laminitis, Navicular disease, Quitter, Sandcrack, Canker and Oestitis!. It was vital we knew how to treat colic, and how to recognise some other diseases such as strangles, tetanus and pneumonia. We had a lot of fun learning all this detail, but I found the ordinary day-to-day management harder to learn. I think this was because one had really to understand the whole horse and its needs. We worked out a schedule for the day – 7 a.m. quarters muck out, pick out feet, check that food is eaten, water, give hay, quick brush and feed, and so on for the rest of the day until the final 10 p.m. check and hay net. It made us realise the amount of work, expense and dedication it takes to own a horse and care for it properly. We practised putting on rugs and applying bandages. We learned about brushing and over-reaching, forging and undercutting and tried to remember how to recognise splint, spavin and sprains.

Part of the Gold Award involves, 'being of valued assistance to other disabled riders'. This is quite hard to fulfil. We encourage each other, but it is hard to be of real assistance, when our walking and balancing is a problem. We would love to be able to help others to tack up, or help others mount, but this is impossible. However, I was not to be allowed to escape from this involvement. One day I was asked to take and instruct a class of five riders, all of whom were mentally handicapped. Under the watchful eyes of many helpers, I walked out into the centre of the field, The riders were walking slowly round, each with a helper leading. Fortunately my voice can be loud and clear, so there was no problem over being heard. I smiled broadly, took a deep breath to counter my nerves, and began the 'lesson' first by introducing myself. I asked them all to halt, and asked each rider his name.

"Now gather up your reins, and ask your horse to walk on, that's right, say it clearly. Try to keep your horse bright and alert. Keep your hands down Jimmy – well done! That looks good Tony, try to sit up straight. Now all of you ask your horse to halt, and feel on the reins. Nice and clear. Very good Simon, you say halt. Now Arthur, try a little trot – could we have another helper please? That's right, up down up down, very good . . . " and so I continued: I was rather enjoying it now, but found the

80

need constantly to turn round to face the riders difficult. It was hard trying to give good simple instructions one at a time so that they could be understood, and to remember always to praise and encourage. I didn't feel I would make a good instructor as there was so much to think about at once. If I concentrated on one rider, I forgot there were another four horses and riders to watch – anything can happen with horses, and instructors need eyes in the back of their head. Eventually Anthea rescued me and helped me back to the others where I was unmercifully teased, and reminded that I had not once changed the rein.

The following week we spent in trying to understand fully the meaning of riding on the correct diagonal and cantering on a named leg. We had tried to learn it all in theory, but actually to apply our knowledge was a very different proposition. I found it hard to think out which fore leg was leading, when one needed all one's attention to keep balanced, steer the horse and give aids. Now we had to feel how the horse was moving, preferably without looking down at the horse's shoulders to check! So we needed to rise when the inside fore leg was leading, and sit when the outside fore leg was leading. I found it all rather confusing, but appreciated how necessary it was to ride on the correct diagonal in order to develop a well balanced horse. When I got it right it felt good. Next we learned to change the rein, and change the diagonal by 'sitting' an extra step. We tried figure-of-eight movements, changing the diagonal with each change of rein. Another problem was to remember to change the stick into the inside hand at the same time.

We then went on to attempt to canter on a named leg. Asking for canter on a bend, when the inside fore leg was leading – it all sounded fine in theory, but in practice I seemed often to get it wrong. I was certainly aware once I'd got the canter on the correct leg as the horse's movement felt smooth and flowing, while on the wrong leg it felt bumpy and strange. The difficulty was again that of trying to do so much at once. As disabled riders, even giving aids to trot need to be thought about. I can't really feel my feet when I ride, so closing the legs on the girth has to be done by putting pressure through my knees. If I don't do this, my toes drop down and my legs flex up, therefore losing a good position. The effort of a sustained trot, or even a short canter, make my legs shake uncontrollably, further masking aids and disturbing balance. In this I know I speak for other riders as well as myself. Backache, blurred vision, and cramped hands may add to our difficulties. Now we were being asked to study the horse's movement and to ride on the correct leg! I have to admit I found this almost impossible, and just hoped our examiner wouldn't make too much of this failure on the day.

Two special days were planned for the Cobbes Meadow group. The first was a picnic and riding to be held in the superb setting of Denne Hill where Caroline our secretary lived. The other was a dressage competition to be held on the following day, also at Denne Hill. The dressage competition involved many groups from around East Kent, and when we arrived late in the morning, the area was thronging with helpers, horses and riders. There were two arenas marked out, and judging was already in progress for various classes of competition.

I greeted Charles who had already ridden. He felt his dressage had gone well, but was disappointed not to be riding the harder dressage test. Recently Charles had had a bad fall, and it was felt wiser to play safe today. Dee was to ride at 12.50 on Sherry, Peter next on Abbey and finally me on Sherry – all in the same class. Dee warmed up on Sherry and then entered the arena once the judges' car horn sounded. She looked good and followed the various manoeuvres well. Peter entered next on Abbey and did extremely well considering the enormous difficulties he has to face. I had mounted Sherry and had allowed myself a brief warm up with Carol staying with me for safety. I felt quite nervous and far more tense than usual. The judges indicated they were ready for me. I asked Sherry to trot, and entered at 'A' at a working trot. Halt and salute at 'A', I remembered to take my time over this, and smiled broadly at the judges thinking it might soften their hearts a little! Working trot now on the right rein and a twenty metre circle at 'B'. I checked the shape of my circle carefully and tried to bend Sherry round correctly. It all seemed to be happening so quickly. Trot round to 'K' walk to 'E' and half circle round to rejoin the track at 'K' – that all felt all right, then canter between 'A' and 'F' right round to 'K'. The canter felt all wrong to me. Was it my nerves, or Sherry being awkward, or were we on the wrong leg? Should I pull Sherry back and ask for canter again or risk it – by now we were nearly at 'K' so it was too late! My legs began to ache and shake. Trot round to 'B' – I noticed Jenny out of the corner of my eye and hoped I wasn't disgracing myself! Circle at 'B' trot to 'H' – I cornered badly, feeling tired now. Walk, half circle, then trot and ask for canter between 'C' and 'M'. This canter felt much better, but again I cut in at the corners, and felt a bit hectic as we cantered round to 'M' across to 'X', trotted up centre line at 'A' – and I must have been

I asked Sherry to trot, and entered at 'A' at a working trot.

four feet off centre line as I came to a shaky, hot, sweaty halt at 'G', managed a salute and breathless smile and walked out of the arena on a long rein at 'A'. I made much of Sherry – always dependable – and asked Anthea about that first canter. She felt it had been all right, so now we had to wait and see!

Charles and I sat on the grass and swopped notes about dressage. I was very shaky and didn't really feel too well, extra anti-spasmodic drugs probably adding to my tiredness. After a while Liz came over to us – "You've both got firsts – well done!" We felt relieved and pleased. Charles had done exceptionally well with an amazing ninety-one marks. I had managed seventy-one with Dee and Peter close behind. A happy prize-giving with Charles making it quite clear that all credit should go to helpers and horses, and we collected our red rosettes. It had been a good day, but Charles and I felt bothered. We had both won our classes, but both felt uneasy, Charles because of his recent fall had had to enter an easier class, and felt he had an advantage over other riders as he had more experience and more knowledge than others in his class. I felt pleased personally that I'd battled with my present problems and entered at all, but that it wasn't really right that I should be competing against Peter, who had far greater difficulties than I. It really poses a problem for RDA as to how to obtain really meaningful competition for their more advanced riders. Discussing this with Catherine later, I explained I would rather have come last in a dressage competition for able-bodied riders than first at that RDA dressage. We all enjoy competition, and this day at Denne Hill had been most enjoyable and worthwhile. Riders from all over East Kent had taken part, and all credit and thanks must go to the organisers of these events. The looks of triumph on disabled children's faces as they collected their rosettes made it all worthwhile, and perhaps only the riders themselves, or dedicated parents could appreciate the individual problems which each rider had to overcome to be able to ride at all.

Before leaving Denne Hill I collected my dressage sheet to read the judges' comments. Listed were all my failings, 'Good entry, halt not square' (obviously the smile didn't help!). 'Circle a little small. Broke canter at 'H'. Late to walk but circle better this time. Cut in at 'M' and broke, but corrected. Overshot at 'A' – little off centre at halt' (I would have said very much off centre!). The final comments were very fair. 'Quite a nice test. Inclined to cut in at corners and not have sufficient inward bend. A good position in the saddle and a very good effort indeed and nice to see seat aids being used'. I had to smile at the last comments as I'm not convinced I was using seat aids or just shifting about as I felt uncomfortable, Plenty of room for improvement I told myself; but my three young boys were very proud of mum's new rosette which now hangs in the lounge!

Chapter Eight

TRIPLE GOLD

Long before I joined Cobbes Meadow group there was a disabled rider named Pat. I want to tell you about Pat, as she was the first rider in the group to attain her Gold Award. Our paths crossed briefly when I started riding just as Pat was leaving to move to another county.

Pat was brought up in Lincolnshire. She had a happy busy childhood, and was always active, living life to the full and enjoying every minute. At the age of seven years she went to boarding school, and it soon became apparent that Pat was to excel at sports. As she grew up through her teenage years she played tennis and went riding. She was strong and athletic, and won several cups. Riding was her first love, and one day when Pat was just sixteen, she and a companion took horses out to prepare them for a hunt the following day. They rode along a bridle way, and at one stage Pat rode her horse at a gallop in advance of her friend. Tragically a local farmer forgot about the riders, and had turned out several sheep, stretching sheep netting across the lane. Not anticipating any dangers, Pat galloped straight into the netting. She was not thrown clear, and the fallen horse rolled on to her. She was rushed to hospital with severe head injuries and remained unconscious for nine days, nearly dying. Pat pulled through and came off the danger list, but it was only then on the eleventh day that the full horror of Pat's injuries became apparent. She was paralysed from the neck down and had broken her back. A surgeon operated, and wonderfully managed to obtain full use in Pat's arms. After a year in hospital Pat could manage to walk four steps with callipers and crutches. She was transferred to Stoke Mandeville hospital, where she stayed for eight months; on her discharge Pat could walk, but very unsteadily and required the use of her wheelchair.

Pat is not a person to give up. The shattering experience of the accident felt like a bad dream, and had a feel of unreality about it, but Pat was too busy working hard to get better to be dragged down by it. She desperately wanted to please her family who were a wonderful support, and she pushed herself to make progress. Pat kept a diary, and noted every small bit of improvement, and this encouraged her and kept her optimistic about the future. Once home, Pat studied for and passed two 'O' level exams, and undertook a shorthand typing course. It so happened that a lady needed a secretary to help with a horse lovers' agency near Oxford, and had asked at Stoke Mandeville if there was anyone suitable. Pat jumped at the job, and soon became a very dear friend of Moyra who ran the agency. Moyra encouraged Pat to try riding again, but Pat was hesitant; she wanted to be quite independent, and not require assistance. She tried sitting on one of the agency ponies, and to her delight discovered she could sit, walk and even trot unsupported. Pat was thrilled, and even bought one of the agency ponies. Her dream was to start jumping, but Moyra insisted Pat bought a special jumping saddle. Luck came Pat's way – she won fifty pounds the next day, and went to London to buy the new saddle! Pat's life now blossomed. She was encouraged to travel, and spent six months touring Europe. She learnt German and arrived back a far more independent and confident person – now walking with the aid of two sticks. Next came a training to become a social worker for the blind, and at twenty-one Pat passed her final exam. There followed two years in Sussex as a social worker where she married and had two lovely children, Tim and Vanda.

When Pat was twenty-eight she moved to Kent. She was a good friend of Lynne (who later became the RDA instructor). Through Lynne, Pat heard that the Cobbes Meadow group were now taking adults, and so Pat was able to start regular riding at Waltham. It was on an RDA riding holiday in Pembrokeshire that Pat first learned about the proficiency tests, and in one holiday she worked for and passed the first four separate Felt tests. She returned the following year to take her Bronze Award. The Silver Award was taken back at Cobbes Meadow on Cocoa, with Catherine and Tricia helping. Having gained Silver, Pat never dreamed she could go on to take Gold, mainly because she didn't feel she could jump. It was at the Spastics Gymkhana at the Royal Mews that Pat went in for a jumping competition – she came equal bottom, but it made her believe she could jump with extra coaching, and so Gold became a possibility. Pat was very excited at the prospect of taking Gold, and practised her jumping a great deal. She rode Dreamer, but just two weeks before she was due to take Gold Award, Dreamer stumbled and went down – mercifully Dreamer rolled over away from Pat, but Pat had still managed to crack some ribs, and Gold had to be postponed! Some weeks later, and after further studying, Pat took the Gold Award. She was asked to ride out in the field and show the examiner all she could do, Catherine rode with her. Pat showed her knowledge of diagonals, changes, aids and jumping. During the questions on stable management, she was showing the examiner a bucket of feed, and out jumped a little mouse!

Pat passed her Gold Award and felt absolutely over the moon. Princess Anne presented her with the award at the headquarters of RDA at the annual general meeting. Shortly afterwards, Pat moved to Wiltshire to give her children Tim and Vanda better educational opportunities. Both children are doing very well, and they are happy in Wiltshire, although Pat misses all her friends from Cobbes Meadow. Pat says that RDA took her back into the world in which she felt at home and comfortable – the world of horses. It transformed her life and gave her new aims and ambitions. She felt she could hold her head up high and forget the restrictions of disability. Pat gives as much as she gets, and is now on the examiners' council and the holiday committee of the RDA.

With only two weeks to go before our Gold exam, it was a real pleasure to see Lynne up at Cobbes Meadow one Tuesday morning. She had come up to give us some final coaching, and the first thing she asked was did we understand the meaning of a well-balanced horse? Blank looks surrounded her, especially from me, as I really hadn't any idea, this topic seemed to have completely passed me by. Lynne explained how a horse naturally balanced itself in the wild. The head is always in front of the forefeet, and is extended as the horse's stride increases. Once a rider is on the horse, the horse's balance has to be adjusted through the head and neck, in distributing weight. A horse develops muscles especially in the back and hind legs through exercising on the level, up and down hills and circling and jumping, and through this development balance is acquired. Lynne paused, had we really understood? She continued, and said it was vital that the horse must be able to have a free forward-going movement and to be able to use himself with the greatest efficiency. Unless a horse is well balanced, he will not be properly collected. The horse should have impulsion in the hind legs, his whole energy collected into a shortened form with a soft mouth on a light rein, so he has maximum control over his limbs and is ready to respond instantly to any aids given. Lynne had explained it so well I felt I understood, and we talked about balance together. Once home I read all I could about it, and thought out the meaning of balance and collection. I felt very thankful to Lynne as I had certainly neglected this area of study.

The telephone rang. It was Anthea, "Would you like to bring the family down for a barbecue and take the horses to the sea?" It was a bright warm day, and soon we were on our way to the coast. When we arrived at Anthea's both Polly and Sherry were brought up to the yard and tied up. The boys helped to carry the tack and soon the horses were ready for a ride. Maurice took the boys down to the bay where we were to meet up. I mounted Sherry with considerable help from Anthea, and she mounted Polly. The horses were keen and fresh, eager to move. We set off down the road with the crisp echoing sound of the horses' hooves beneath us. Sherry knew this ride well and needed no encouragement to go forward. Ahead of us were the tufted sand dunes of the bay, sculptured into strange hollowed shapes. We turned the horses into the wind and rode at a steady trot along the edge of the bay. Sherry pulled hard and I needed all my wits about me as we wound our way up and down and round over the sand dunes.

The irregular paces of the horses required a light seat and good balance, keeping steady contact with the mouth. It reminded me of the ride in Yorkshire so many years ago now, when the sturdy little fell ponies had almost leapt from crag to crag. My riding skills had undoubtedly advanced since these early rides, but now my muscles were weak and unco-ordinated. Anthea encouraged me to follow her down across the flat sand to the sea. The pale, clear water rolled in small, gentle waves on to the sand. The boys were playing nearby and waved enthusiastically as we rode by. Sherry wasn't so sure about going into the water, and Anthea told me to feel on the right rein and use my legs to encourage her. Into the water we went, the horses' hooves splashing enthusiastically. Polly and Sherry were loving this paddle, and it was all I could do to hold Sherry back or I'm sure she would have taken off and cantered away, The wind flew through the horses' manes and tails, making them fly and flutter in the breeze.

Eventually we headed the horses up and back across the beach, Sherry pulling strongly now, sensing the homeward track. I felt excited at the freedom of the ride, and the power with which Sherry carried me. Sand is almost impossible to walk on when one has difficulties walking, and wheelchairs just sink! Sherry was taking me carefully in the water and over the sand, and it was a wonderful experience. We turned on to the road, and then up along a soft grassy track beside fields full of crops. The wind had dropped as we had left the sea, and the warmth of the sun seeped through my shirt on to my back. I felt exhilarated, and thrilled with the sheer bliss of this ride. Sherry was strong to handle, but I felt safe as Anthea kept a careful eye on us. The land was flat and the fields stretched out as far as one could see, offering their wheat and barley to the sun. A stream flowed quietly by and we followed its course. Not a sound disturbed the peace of the fields except the quiet thud of the hooves on the soft grass. My body moved easily with Sherry's rhythm. I looked into the clear sky and thought how easy it felt compared to walking when legs were stiff and awkward and balance poor. I would pull one reluctant heavy leg after the other, and prop myself up with my stick. Here, on Sherry there was a natural freedom of movement, a smoothness and a strength in which I rejoiced.

Maurice and the boys were already at Anthea's when we returned. Tim and Chris helped to care for the horses and young Jon assisted with the barbecue. We sat on wooden seats in the peace of a beautiful garden. Long cool drinks, beefburgers and sausages were much appreciated by all. After lunch we took the horses down to a nearby field. It was the boys' turn to enjoy a ride now. Tim already had a little experience of riding and could manage a rising trot. Chris had never ridden, but had a natural seat. Jon clung on and just enjoyed himself. As usual Sherry took each one of her novice riders with that special care and patience unique to her. Time now to take the horses down to their grazing land. Tim rode Sherry and a friend of Anthea's took Polly. We turned the horses out into their familiar pastures and, with a shake and a kick of glee, they were off, released from their responsibilities and allowed their freedom. It had been a beautiful day, a delight for each one of us, and we thanked Anthea for her kindness with happy hearts as we turned for home.

I woke with a start "Come on Mummy, time to wake up." Jon was already dressed and ready for school. Slowly it dawned on me – today was the big day we had worked for over the past four years. Today was the exam for the RDA Gold Award. Could we possibly succeed? Could we possibly bring more Gold Awards to Cobbes Meadow and follow Pat's lead? I dressed quickly into my jodhpurs, white shirt and burgundy tie. I had recently bought a new jockey crash cap and wore it with a burgundy silk to match. After breakfast and many 'good lucks' from the

Into the water we went, the horses' hooves splashing.

family, I drove up to the school. Too late to learn anything now, it was simply a matter of keeping calm, and hoping our examiners treated us gently!

Charles was his usual calm cheery self, while Pam was very nervous and I felt pretty jittery. There would be two examiners, and all three sections, dressage, jumping and theory would be taken at the school. A car drew up, it was the examiners. I mounted Sherry and warmed up a little in the field, feeling tense now and wishing it was all over. The examiners came and watched me. I felt a bit confused, had we begun or was I still warming up? After a while Anthea told me to ride various figures.

The gentleman examiner called over to me, "What are you trying to do madam?" I rode up to him, relieved to see a broad smile on his face and a certain twinkle in his eye.

"I'm trying to execute a change," I shakily replied, attempting to sound very professional.

"All right, do it again, and just do your own thing, show me what you can do." I hadn't bargained for freedom like this and felt pleased. I walked round the field, trying to keep Sherry alert and active, with good forward going movement and impulsion. I halted, counted six seconds then reined back three paces, and forward again. Next I asked Sherry for a trot, and performed a figure of eight hoping desperately I was on the correct diagonal, and sitting a pace as I changed the diagonal and the rein. When my right hand developed a cramp through my thumb, I knew it had been unwise to ride with a stick, and I quickly handed it to Anthea. No questions were asked so I continued with a rising trot and a twenty metre circle, before I asked for a canter on the right rein. Sherry felt good and I was confident we were on the correct leg. Back to trot across the centre, and another canter on the left rein. I felt tense and again that feeling of being a bit 'hectic' as if it was all happening too quickly. My cornering, as usual, had been poor, and my transitions felt rough and unsteady but the examiner was still beaming, so I decided enough was enough and came to a halt. My legs were shaking already and I feared I wouldn't manage the jumping. Pam and Charles were nowhere to be seen and I wondered how they were getting on.

At this stage the lady examiner appeared and asked me what I understood by a well-balanced horse. Oh, how glad I was for that last minute revision with Lynne! I recounted all I knew, trying to make it all sound very familiar, as if I'd known the meaning of a well-balanced horse all my life! The lady seemed well pleased, and I was asked to dismount, which I did with the aid of two helpers in my usual rather ungainly style, and walked back into the annexe of the school where I sat in a wheelchair for a brief rest. I thought Pam was in the school as I could hear something going on there, and I caught a glimpse of Charles going out to the field. It was lovely that the three of us were all trying for Gold together. We were good friends, and we had struggled and laughed our way through the previous months with a delightful sense of team spirit. Now the moment of truth had arrived, and we desperately hoped we could all either pass or fail – for one to fail or succeed alone would be a cruel blow to us all.

It was my turn to jump. I mounted Sherry, dear old Sherry, who had always been so faithful and so obliging. We entered the indoor school. There were nine jumps set out, all different, some double jumps, some crossed poles, all set at between two and three foot high. The gentleman examiner told me to walk the course on Sherry, and then jump in my own time. I nervously glanced at Anthea, who returned a reassuring smile. I examined each jump carefully and tried to calculate how steep a turn I would need to make in order to face the next jump. Each jump was no different than I had jumped before, but never had I tried to jump nine jumps consecutively. I was ready now, and the examiner nodded for me to begin.

I asked Sherry to trot on, then to canter before the first jump. Up and over, no problems there, then followed another before a steep turn, so far so good. Jump number three was a double, and that went well, but I hardly seemed to regain my pace before the next jump, and a rougher landing. Without breaking the canter jumps five and six were satisfactory, but now my legs were aching with the effort and began to shake. I cantered up the long side taking one more crossed pole jump but the landing was heavy. Next I needed to turn sharply to get to the correct angle. Sherry bent round but in a flash she stumbled slightly. It was just enough to throw me up on the crest. I hung on feeling I was going to fall. Sherry steadied and I faltered, not sure if I could pull my weak body back into the saddle. I heard the examiner, or Anthea or someone say "go on," and I managed to straighten myself. I shook terribly but asked again for canter and jumped the following double jump. One more to go, but I felt I had little control left over my tired shaky muscles this one was up to Sherry. She cantered steadily and leapt smoothly over the final jump, landing more gently than ever. Convinced Sherry knew exactly what she was doing to help me, I almost wept with relief as I made much of her. Anthea looked delighted, and the examiner came over and congratulated me for handling the stumble so well, but I knew it was thanks to Sherry we had managed to stay the course.

As I rested in the annexe in my wheelchair, I felt a sense of careless abandon. Two sections of the exam were completed. I did not know how the others were doing, but I knew that I couldn't have done any more. I had given all I had in physical strength, and now, feeling exhausted, I had to face the daunting thought of the theory exam.

Pam and Charles came and joined me, and we chatted intently over a cup of coffee. Charles felt as I did – we had done the best we could and it was too late to change anything now. Pam felt anxious but agreed her riding had probably been up to standard. Pam's riding had always been very good, the theory worried her more, as she found it so hard to remember facts. The two examiners now indicated they were ready for us and, to our surprise, all three of us were to be examined together, around the entrance to the stable. We sat in our wheelchairs feeling very tired and waited for the first question. Just as we had thought, it was the everyday care of a horse that the examiners questioned us on. They insisted on hearing the daily routine in detail. Nothing was to be left out. What feeds, in exactly what amounts would we give and why? When and how would we groom, water and muck out? What type of bedding would we use and why? What would we check the horse for? How would we know if the horse had pneumonia? What was the normal rate of respiration and the normal temperature? The questions were directed to each of us in turn. Charles was direct and steady with his answers – he gave me confidence. Pam was more hesitant, but was remembering facts and names well. I was answering fully (waffling I call it) trying to lead the examiner on to ground I knew we felt safe on!

I was asked about the ailments of the foot. I reeled off several names, feeling fairly sure of myself, and suggested forms of treatment. It was a mistake. The examiner sensed my confidence, but said I had left out one thing. I thought carefully, but could think of nothing. He insisted there was something I should have done. Something important. My confidence melted away as I looked into his enquiring eyes. "You've forgotten to get a tetanus injection done!" he bellowed at me, with that same broad grin we had seen before. I got the distinct impression he was enjoying himself. We ceased to notice the time or Anthea almost bursting with frustration if we hesitated over an answer. We stopped feeling tired. We ceased to count the questions. The whole exam became an intense discussion on the care of a horse; training, feeding, stabling, tack, shoeing and recognising and treating ailments. At long last the questions came to a halt. We had been sitting there for an hour and a half!

The examiners now walked away together into the school. We sat in silence, then quietly tried to reassure each other over various answers given. We felt so tired, as if we were in some kind of vacuum. After several minutes the examiners strode firmly back towards us. A broad smile, and a hand extended to shake ours – and a rich deep voice saying "Congratulations to each of you, you've all passed your Gold Award." I looked at Charles, Pam, Anthea, and swallowed hard to shift the lump which had suddenly come to my throat. We were all so tired, so relieved, so thankful we hardly knew what to feel or say. Three more Gold Awards for Cobbes Meadow. I thought of Jenny and how thrilled she would be; of Lynne, Catherine and so many helpers who had never ceased their encouragement and help. I thought back on the long revisions at Anthea's and Catherine's homes, of Anthea's groom, Pauline, and the special instructors who had visited to teach some new skill. I thought of Maurice and our three boys. We thanked the examiners, and soon set off for home. On the way back through Canterbury we stopped at a florist and ordered an arrangement of all gold flowers to be sent to Anthea with a little note:

Thanks for Gold
Charles, Pam and Pennie.

The summer was now upon us and after some delightful relaxed and carefree rides, we said our farewells as we left for the summer break. Pam had been told many months ago that she needed an operation to replace the knee on her good leg – as strain over the years had caused damage. She had refused surgery until after the Gold exam, but now went into hospital as advised. The operation went well, but since then Pam has been unable to bend her leg, and following surgery she suffered a mild stroke which affected her sight. She certainly couldn't have taken the Gold exam in this condition, so we all felt it was marvellous she had postponed the operation. Charles left for a holiday feeling well satisfied with life, and Maurice and I had a few days away, while our boys were at scout camp. I felt very happy and so pleased for Cobbes Meadow. They had given us so much and it was wonderful to feel we could give a little back. Late in August, Maurice and I took our lads away to Wales for a ten day holiday. However, after only two days away I developed a severe cough and cold with a high temperature. I felt rotten, especially as I didn't want to spoil the holiday for the family. Throughout that holiday I continued to feel ill and depressed. I was so anxious an infection might spark off a relapse of the multiple sclerosis. On return home I saw my doctor, and we realised my legs had become stiff and heavy. Over the following two months I continued to feel unwell, and felt I was slipping downhill. I went to Cobbes Meadow a few times to ride, but felt so weak I could do only very little.

I phoned Anthea and explained I would have to leave riding until things improved. In November, I contracted flu and within two days I had a complete relapse. I developed a spastic paralysis of my left side. I couldn't walk, was unable to unbend my left leg, arm or hand, unable to pass water, and I temporarily lost the sight in one eye. I felt dreadful, and in a lot of pain as I had spasms of the muscles of my left leg. The family were dismayed, as were my friends. Fortunately I had a marvellous doctor and very soon I began a course of Cortisone injections each day. Three consultants visited me at home, and each one said the same – that they were sure I would recover and feel well again, but that I would have to be patient and put up with the unpleasant side-effects of the Cortisone.

My eye was the first to recover for within a week the vision began to improve and by ten days the sight was almost normal, with no lasting deterioration. The next several weeks were very hard. People in the parish were fantastic. They organised hot meals to be brought to the rectory for all the family every other evening, and a special tasty dish for me each lunch time. Friends would call in and sit with me and encourage me. The district nurses were marvellous, coming in each morning and evening to treat, make comfortable and encourage. I wondered if I would be able to ride again or whether my luck had eventually run out. I missed riding greatly, but kept in contact with friends from RDA. My physiotherapist Dudley, who was so caring, was impressed by the lack of muscle wasting and was sure this was because of my regular riding. The Cortisone made me put on an enormous amount of weight, and my face puffed out with the 'mooning' effect of Cortisone.

Maurice and our three boys were tremendous. How Maurice coped with me as well as the parish and the boys I shall never know. He was never despondent but always positive that I would recover. The boys would come home from school and help the nurses tidy my room, make drinks, help with the ironing; they were super and I shall always feel proud of them. Just before Christmas there was some vague improvement, and it was arranged I should go by ambulance to the local hospital for further physiotherapy and hydrotherapy. I had been in bed for two months and was terribly weak, but gradually muscles unclenched and I began to walk again with crutches.

I knew the presentation of our Gold Awards was to be sometime in January, and I so hoped to be able to go. As for riding, I daren't think that far. I really couldn't believe I could ride again but I felt determined to make a return to riding my goal. Over the next few weeks I fought to walk again, utterly determined not to give up! Everyone who came to me was so kind and determined with me that I felt carried along with their enthusiasm. At times the struggle felt too much and I would be overwhelmed with tears, only to pick myself up again and go forward. I was now allowed downstairs again, and gradually came off the Cortisone and the powerful anti-spasmodic drugs. My weight began to subside again, and twice-weekly physiotherapy at the hospital helped weak unco-ordinated muscles to come together again. The presentation was to be on January 24th and I began to feel I could be well enough by then. It had been a long haul; I felt I had missed the winter as suddenly we were looking forward to spring with all its potential of new life and warmth.

Pam was now out of hospital and recovering from her problems. I was up and walking again and improving with amazing speed. Charles was well, and so it was that we met up for the presentation of our awards. We had hoped that Princess Anne would be able to present the Gold Awards, but because of her hectic schedule that was not possible, but we were disappointed. However, in true Cobbes Meadow style, everything was done to give us a very special presentation, which was to be performed by the Lord Lieutenant of Kent at his beautiful home near Sittingbourne.

We met in Canterbury and clambered aboard a special coach. There was much chat and laughter as cases of food, drink and glasses were pushed inside the coach. It was good to see so many friends again, Charles, Pam, Peter and Stephen were all there and Catherine, Caroline, Sonia, Tricia, Anthea and Liz, and many other helpers and relatives of the riders. The Mayor's car led the way, and we followed, out through the city and into the country, eventually winding our way down little country lanes, which our driver declared were far too narrow for his coach! Soon we entered the magnificent grounds of the Lord Lieutenant's home, looking stately and proud amongst grand lawns and huge spreading trees. We were met by the Lord Lieutenant (looking resplendent in full uniform including spurs) and his charming wife, and the Mayor who had been kind enough to be with us for this day. Peter, who had examined us for some of our tests, was there, and Alex Bennett and Jenny. After introductions we were shown into a beautiful room where we were served champagne and marvellous eats – all prepared and brought by the helpers of Cobbes Meadow. I could hardly believe it was all happening. The past four years of friendship and fun, memories of fantastic rides, falls, studying and through it all the steady care and commitment of the helpers and organisers. It seemed crazy that we were here to receive awards – when my whole feeling was to give all praise to Cobbes Meadow.

Next the presentation took place. The Lord Lieutenant made a speech and said how pleased and proud he was to be giving the awards. Peter and Stephen who have shown such enormous courage in the face of huge problems received their Bronze Awards. Then Pam was asked to go and receive her Gold Award. It felt great to see Pam so happy. This had been her final chance to take Gold as she had to have further surgery. She had so desperately wanted to pass, and now, along with splints, plasters and wheelchair, she was receiving the award. As the clapping died down, Charles was asked to come forward. I knew that under that broad smile and kind face was a very determined and courageous man. The number of times I had seen Charles fall, reach for his glasses, dust himself down and remount made me feel full of admiration for him. We had shared our ups and downs, allowed each other a few minutes' moan time, and then encouraged each other to get on with the task in hand. Well done, Charles.

Now my name was called. I looked quickly at Maurice at my side and wanted him to come with me – I couldn't have gained this award without his continued encouragement and support. Walking slowly up to the Lord Lieutenant I noticed Jenny, Catherine and Anthea, and wanted to share this moment with them, for they had given so much. I shook hands, and received the gold badge and certificate, and the beautiful engraved shield. It all seemed unbelievable.

Riding for the Disabled had added a new dimension to my life just at a time when horizons seemed to be shrinking, doors closing and all kinds of possibilities fading away. It hurt to be disabled, but riding had taken away much of that hurt and replaced it with adventure, fun and achievement. As I looked at my Cobbes Meadow friends I knew I was saying, along with hundreds of other disabled folk all over the country, "Thank you for bringing hope, confidence and trust into my life."

POSTSCRIPT

Following the opening of the new indoor riding school in 1984, it was felt that a safe seated area was required overlooking the arena. Subsequently, in 1986, a raised viewing gallery was built to accommodate spectators, riders waiting to ride, and for use on open days and instruction days. Water sprinklers were also fitted to dampen the floor to restrict dust.

In 1994 the Linnet Room was opened. Built immediately adjacent to the school, this gives a warm room where riders and helpers can enjoy tea and coffee, and relax in soft chairs and benefit from rest, discussion or teaching. The room was built partly from generous donations given in memory of Alex, our president, and Carol, one of our most loved and respected helpers, who gave us the impetus to start our fund-raising campaign.

Cobbes Meadow now accommodates various riding groups from Monday to Friday each week. Riders continue to enter RDA tests and exams, and have competed sucessfully at the leading Regional RDA Championships at various venues including Arundel, Hickstead, and Hever leading to successes at the National Championships at Moreton Morell, Stoneleigh. The Driving Group has completed successfully at Windsor and Ascot, in the British Driving Society Show, and one of our members won the Cross Country Driving Competition at Bradbourne.

At present there are some two hundred riders and seventy-five helpers at Cobbes Meadow, with many more riders on the waiting list. More helpers are needed in order that this magnificent work may continue to bring mental and physical benefit to so many disabled riders.

A percentage of the royalties from the sale of this book will be given to Cobbes Meadow.